Partakers of the Life Divine

Partakers of the Life Divine

Participation in the Divine Nature
in the Writings of Charles Wesley

※

S T Kimbrough, Jr.

FOREWORD BY
Peter Bouteneff

CASCADE *Books* · Eugene, Oregon

PARTAKERS OF THE LIFE DIVINE
Participation in the Divine Nature in the Writings of Charles Wesley

Copyright © 2016 S T Kimbrough, Jr. All rights reserved. Except for brief quotations in critical publications or reviews, no part of this book may be reproduced in any manner without prior written permission from the publisher. Write: Permissions, Wipf and Stock Publishers, 199 W. 8th Ave., Suite 3, Eugene, OR 97401.

Cascade Books
An Imprint of Wipf and Stock Publishers
199 W. 8th Ave., Suite 3
Eugene, OR 97401

www.wipfandstock.com

PAPERBACK ISBN: 978-1-4982-0189-6
HARDCOVER ISBN: 978-1-4982-8682-4
EBOOK ISBN: 978-1-4982-0190-2

Cataloguing-in-Publication data:

Names: Kimbrough, S. T., 1936– |

Title: Partakers of the life divine : participation in the divine nature in the writings of Charles Wesley / S T Kimbrough, Jr. ; foreword by Peter Bouteneff.

Description: Eugene, OR: Cascade Books, 2016 | Includes bibliographical references and index(es).

Identifiers: ISBN 978-1-4982-0189-6 (paperback) | ISBN 978-1-4982-8682-4 (hardcover) | ISBN 978-1-4982-0190-2 (ebook)

Subjects: LCSH: Wesley, Charles, 1707–1788—Contributions in doctrine of sanctification. | Wesley, Charles, 1707–1788. | Deification (Christianity)

Classification: BT765.W45 K56 2016 (print) | BT765.W45 K56 (ebook)

Manufactured in the U.S.A.   JUNE 22, 2016

This volume is dedicated to the late Father Thomas Hopko, Orthodox visionary, New Testament scholar, and former Dean of St. Vladimir's Orthodox Theological Seminary in Crestwood, New York, whose welcoming spirit, keen insight, and friendship motivated this author's continued exploration of the subject addressed in this volume.

Tri-une God, the New-Creator
    Of our fallen souls appear,
O communicate thy nature,
    Raise us to thy image *here*,
In true holiness renewed,
Spotless portraitures of God.

—CHARLES WESLEY

Contents

Foreword by Peter Bouteneff ix

Abbreviations xiii

Technical Matters xv

Introduction 1

1: Background: Charles Wesley's Theology of Mystery 8

2: Prose Sources: Journal and Sermons 16

3: The Life Divine and Participation in the Divine Nature 25

4: The Incarnation and Participation in the Divine Nature 37

5: The Sacraments and Participation in the Divine Nature 45

6: The Trinity and Participation in the Divine Nature 61

7: The Church and Participation in the Divine Nature 74

8: Divine Love and Participation in the Divine Nature 87

9: Illumination and Participation in the Divine Nature 101

10: Transfiguration and Participation in the Divine Nature 113

11: Sanctification and Participation in the Divine Nature 122

12: Participation in the Divine Nature as Progression 128

13: Evaluating Charles Wesley's Views of Participation in the Light of the Early Church Fathers 136

Epilogue: The *Philokalia* and the Charles Wesley Corpus 149

Selected Bibliography 151

Index of Personal Names 159

Index of Scripture Passages 162

Index of Subjects 165

Foreword

During points in the mid-twentieth century, "deification" became the exclusive Orthodox way of referring to salvation. We would wear it as a badge. We would use the Greek *theosis* in order to insure that it sounded especially impenetrable to the layperson. And it would be ours: Lutherans had Justification, Methodists had Holiness, and Orthodox had *theosis*.[1] It was a bigger, better, and more mystical way of expressing salvation. By making such cynical remarks I do not mean to belittle a teaching that is absolutely right and true, also exquisitely beautiful and genuinely mysterious. Quite to the contrary, I am saying that whenever we Orthodox began to turn *theosis* into a mere identity marker we were in danger of belittling it ourselves.

Yet neither would I want to minimize the genuine differences between Eastern and Western Christian concepts and methods in considering salvation. There is truth to every stereotype, and the one that says that Western theology has tended toward the legalistic and scholastic while Eastern theology is "mystical" and communion-oriented has sometimes and in some ways been true. The number of Western Christian treatises that have sought to identify the recipient/payee of the sacrifice of Christ testifies to this fact, as do the resulting concepts and practices surrounding merits and indulgences, especially in the Latin world. So do the five points of Calvinism.

All of this to say that when Western Christian theologians take up the teaching of deification, as they increasingly have in recent decades, it is a welcome thing. For one, it reveals deification to be a doctrine of universal significance and not a regional or confessional trophy. It also helps dissolve the clichés about how Eastern and Western Christians conceive the theological endeavor generally, and the nature of salvation specifically. And finally it reveals how much Christians from different traditions have to learn from each other. The present book takes its place among several

---

1. On this phenomenon, see, e.g., Kalaitzidis, "The West in Contemporary Greek Theology," 147f.

recent studies that have shown Western Christian traditions to have latent or evident interest in this doctrine.²

That deification should be taken up by many Western Christians is testimony to several overlapping phenomena. One is a common sense of *ressourcement*. During the twentieth century, and more so as that century progressed, theologians East and West, sometimes in league with each other, came to draw on their common forebears of the early church. This came as a recognition that contemporary theology, liturgy, prayer, and Christian life in general could experience a profound enrichment through an engagement with the Church during its formative period. Among Western thinkers it was especially Roman Catholic and Anglican theologians who first came to join Orthodox thinkers—for example, through the Fellowship of St. Alban and St. Sergius—in a spiritual and academic encounter with the first-millennium Church.

But Calvinist and Lutheran theologians have taken their own turn toward the church fathers, largely through a recognition that the Reformers themselves were so deeply impressed by the Fathers through their academic engagement with them. Anglicans, too, saw how reverently theologians such as Lancelot Andrewes harvested from the early church. This same spirit came to life for Methodists who recognized the depth with which the Wesleys read the early church theologians, and how clearly the patristic spirit rang out in their sermons, writings, and hymns.

Apart from this common return *ad fontes*, we have witnessed a more generalized sharing of spiritual gifts among Eastern and Western Christian churches, itself owing to at least two phenomena. One is the ecumenical movement that brought Christians of widely diverse traditions together in the twentieth century after centuries of what, in some cases, had been a nearly complete estrangement. The other is the increase in migration that has brought Eastern Christians into the West, such that Christians of different traditions would find themselves side by side with each other. Although Orthodox Christians were and remain a small minority in the West, neither they nor their Western colleagues would again find it possible to think theologically in isolation from each other.

These encounters have led to a genuine exchange of gifts. Western Christians have received the work of theologians such as Vladimir Lossky, Sergius Bulgakov, Georges Florovsky, Alexander Schmemann, and later, John Zizioulas with enthusiasm. On a more aesthetic and often more

2. The main authors are cited in the early pages of this book's introduction.

FOREWORD

popular level, many Western Christians have warmly welcomed icons and Russian and Byzantine liturgical music into their churches and homes. The Orthodox, as a minority seeking to retain their identity, have thus far not been as obviously receptive to gifts from the West but are rapidly becoming more so. And they have engaged in deep and heartfelt exchanges of resources and wisdom through formal and informal ecumenical encounters.

S T Kimbrough, Jr., is a fine and thoughtful Wesley scholar, and also a major figure in Orthodox-Methodist relations. In recent decades he has organized several meetings of the highest caliber that, bypassing formal ecumenical channels, produced substantial scholarly results, a significant part of the exchange of gifts that it is our joint calling to continue.[3] With this book he is resuming a leadership role in that relationship.

John and Charles Wesley are two of the most important theologians of their millennium. It is all too rarely remembered—even among contemporary Methodists—that their movement of church revival and holiness had a significant grounding in the church fathers. That fact has the added significance of according them a potentially central role in the movement of church rapprochement, especially among those churches that feel especially indebted to the patristic heritage and to a robustly traditional doctrine of God, his Son Jesus Christ, his Holy Spirit, creation, and redemption.

Charles Wesley, the specific subject of the present volume, is of particular significance as one who expressed his theology in poetry of heart-rending beauty and theological gravity. His massive corpus of hymns has seen theological study, but no extensive study on deification until this volume, which the author hopes will stimulate further exploration. Charles Wesley's poetic mind and heart are here shown to yield new insights on this subject, some unique to him even as they are consonant with the tradition. As but one important example, we might take note of the centrality of *love* in Wesley's understanding of deification, a theme to which he frequently returns without it ever growing tired or sentimental. Sometimes it takes a poet to call us back to such fundamental, essential truths about the relationship between God and his beloved human creation.

The Orthodox Church has given the title of "Theologian" to only three of her esteemed saints: John the Evangelist, Gregory of Nazianzus, and Symeon "the New Theologian." I have heard it suggested that the bestowal

---

3. These were published in three volumes by St. Vladimir's Seminary Press, all edited by S T Kimbrough, Jr.: *Orthodox and Wesleyan Spirituality* (2002), *Orthodox and Wesleyan Scriptural Understanding and Practice* (2005), and *Orthodox and Wesleyan Ecclesiology* (2007).

Foreword

of this name had to do with the fact that all three expressed their theology poetically. Another great theological poet, Ephrem the Syrian, would have surely deserved the title on those merits. Might not Charles Wesley as well?

Peter Bouteneff
Feast of Epiphany, 2015
Associate Professor in Systematic Theology
St. Vladimir's Orthodox Theological Seminary
Crestwood, New York

Abbreviations

Abbreviation	Title	Baker Bibliography[1]
Children's Hymns 1763	*Hymns for Children, 1763*	[#223]
Family Hymns 1767	*Hymns for the Use of Families, 1767*	[#245]
Funeral Hymns 1759	*Funeral Hymns, 1759* (enlargement of #115)	[#197]
HGEL 1742	*Hymns on God's Everlasting Love,* 2nd Series, [1742]	[#32]
HLS 1745	*Hymns on the Lord's Supper, 1745*	[#83]
HSP 1739	*Hymns and Sacred Poems, 1739*	[#15]
HSP 1740	*Hymns and Sacred Poems, 1740*	[#19]
HSP 1742	*Hymns and Sacred Poems, 1742*	[#40]
HSP 1749	*Hymns and Sacred Poems, 1749*	[#138]
Nativity Hymns 1745	*Hymns for the Nativity of our Lord, 1745*	[#84]
Pentecost Hymns 1746	*Hymns of Petition and Thanksgiving for the Promise of the Father (Whitsunday Hymns), 1746*	[#92]
Preparation for Death 1772	*Preparation for Death, in Several Hymns, 1772*	[#285]
Redemption Hymns 1747	*Hymns for those that seek and those that have Redemption in the Blood of Jesus Christ, 1747*	[#105]
Resurrection Hymns 1746	*Hymns for Our Lord's Resurrection, 1746*	[#90]
Scripture Hymns 1762	*Short Hymns on Select Passages of the Holy Scriptures, 1762*	[#214]
Trinity Hymns 1767	*Hymns on the Trinity, 1767*	[#246]

1. Baker, *A Union Catalogue.*

Abbreviations

Other Abbreviations

AV/KJV	King James Version of the Bible (1611); Authorized Version of the Church of England
BCP	Book of Common Prayer
MSJ	S T Kimbrough, Jr., and Kenneth G. C. Newport, eds. *The Manuscript Journal of the Rev. Charles Wesley, M. A.* 2 vols. Nashville: Kingswood, 2008.
MSACTS	*Manuscript Acts* (MA 1977/555)[2]
MSLK	*Manuscript Luke* (MA 1977/577)
MSMK	*Manuscript Mark* (MA 1977/574)
MSMT	*Manuscript Matthew* (MA 1977/577)
NPNF	*Nicene and Post-Nicene Fathers of the Christian Church*, Second series. 14 vols. Reprint. Eds. Philip Schaff and Henry Wace. Peabody, MA: Hendrickson, 1994.
PG	J.-P. Migne, ed. *Patrologia graeca.* 161 vols. Paris, 1857–66.
PW	George Osborn, ed. *The Poetical Works of John and Charles Wesley.* 13 vols. London: Wesleyan-Methodist Conference Office, 1868–72.
UP	S T Kimbrough, Jr., and Oliver A. Beckerlegge, eds. *The Unpublished Poetry of Charles Wesley.* 3 vols. Nashville: Kingswood, 1988–92.
Wesley, *Sermons*	Kenneth G. C. Newport, *The Sermons of Charles Wesley: A Critical Edition with Introduction and Notes.* Oxford, UK: Oxford University Press, 2001.
1780 *Collection*	Franz Hildebrandt and Oliver A. Beckerlegge, eds. *A Collection of Hymns for the Use of the People Called Methodists.* Vol. 7 of *The Works of John Wesley.* Nashville: Abingdon, 1983.

---

2. The Accession numbers of the John Rylands Library, Manchester, UK, appear in parenthesis following MSACTS and the abbreviations of the manuscripts for the Gospels of Matthew, Mark, and Luke.

Technical Matters

1. The poems that appear in this volume are quoted from the first editions or printings in which they appeared. If quoted from manuscript copies that is noted. Generally Wesley's spellings are retained; however, verb forms in the past tense are spelled in full, e.g., finish'd = finished; old spellings such as "compleat" are changed to modern spellings, i.e., "complete." The apostrophes used by Wesley when omitting vowels to accommodate poetical meter, e.g., "heav'n" (one syllable in place of two for "heaven") are retained. Original punctuation is generally preserved, but the capitalization of nouns has not been retained except for proper names and places.
2. The poems quoted from *Scripture Hymns* (1762) are usually preceded in the original source by sequential numbers and verses of Scripture. The volume and page number, along with the Scripture reference and text, are given in the footnotes.
3. Original sources and locations of the poems are indicated in the footnotes by abbreviations and short titles or abbreviations of the sources. See the list of abbreviations above.
4. The complete texts of poems, i.e., all stanzas, are not always included here; however, the numbers of the stanzas are usually included in the text or footnotes.
5. Roman numerals usually have been converted to Arabic numerals.
6. The abbreviations and short titles of original sources are utilized in the body of the text and footnotes as they appear in the list of sources above.
7. A few passages from the BCP Psalter used by Wesley are included. Most of the texts quoted from Scripture are from the King James Version of the Bible (1611)/Authorized Version of the Church of England, since it was the text generally used by Charles Wesley and greatly influenced modes of expression in his poetry.

Introduction

Theology couched in poetry is often questionable for those who prefer a prose-expressed theology that fits appropriately into the inheritance of the well-thought-through theology influenced by scholars of central Europe, especially following the patterns of logic, methodology, historical and philosophical analysis of Gotthold Ephraim Lessing (1729–81), Ludwig Wittgenstein (1889–1951), and Martin Heidegger (1889–1976). For theologians of Orthodoxy and for Charles Wesley, however, poetry is one of the most viable modes of theological expression. The contemporary Greek philosopher Christos Yannaras (1935–) has eloquently expressed the value of poetry for Christian theology in his volume *The Elements of Faith*:

> The apophatic attitude leads Christian theology to use the language of poetry and images for the interpretation of dogmas much more than the language of conventional logic and schematic concepts. The conventional logic of everyday understanding can very easily give man a false sense of a sure knowledge which, being won by the intellect, is already exhausted by it, completely possessed by it. While poetry, with the symbolisms and images which it uses, always exhibits a sense from within the words and beyond the words, a concept which corresponds more to common experiences of life and less to cerebral conceptions.[1]

These are important words to bear in mind in this study of the theological concept of participation in the divine nature, which relies heavily on the literature, particularly poetry, of the eighteenth-century poet/priest of the Church of England, Charles Wesley. In such a study the "sense from within the words and beyond the words" is extremely important. Furthermore, Wesley's theology is more poetic than propositional and more experiential than systematic, and thus it exhibits many affinities with the theology of the Eastern Church.

1. Yannaras, *Elements of Faith*, 17.

To Yannaras' words should be added those of A. M. Allchin about the value of hymns as theology: "A true hymn is neither simply a statement of doctrine nor simply an expression of devotion. It is a text in which thought and feeling, imagination and reason, have been fused together by the poet's craft and vision, through the gift of the Holy Spirit."[2]

In an earlier essay, "*Theosis* in the Writings of Charles Wesley," published in *St. Vladimir's Theological Quarterly*,[3] I addressed two areas of his understanding of participation in the divine nature, namely, the incarnation and the Eucharist. The title of the essay was perhaps inappropriate, if one assumes therefrom that Charles Wesley used the word *theosis* in his writings. He did not. This word, a noun coined by St. Gregory of Nazianzus from the Greek verb Θεόω ("to deify"), was used by Gregory and others after him as a synonym for deification.

When the words *theosis* and *deification* appear in this study in connection with Charles Wesley's theology, they are used in the sense of the phrases he uses: "partakers of the life divine" or "participation in/of the life divine." These phrases generally will be understood as equivalents for "deification" and are the preferred expressions in Wesley's theology. It is important to acknowledge, however, the long history of the differences of the use of and preferences for the terms *deification* and *participation* from Origen and St. Athanasius to St. Maximus the Confessor, which can only be addressed here selectively where appropriate. Charles Wesley does not use the word *deification* but he does use the verb *partake* and the noun *participation* in reference to accessing "life divine" and the "divine nature."

We shall see in the course of this study that Norman Russell's definition of *theosis* is extremely helpful for understanding Charles Wesley's views of partaking of the divine nature. "Theosis is our restoration as persons to integrity and wholeness by participation in Christ through the Holy Spirit, in a process which is initiated in this world through our life of ecclesial communion and moral striving and finds ultimate fulfillment in our union with the Father—all within the broad context of the divine economy."[4]

Methodologically it is extremely important to note at the beginning of this work that direct attestation to the influence of the church fathers on Charles Wesley's thought by way of his reading of original sources is not possible. Therefore, the establishment of congruency of thought and

---

2. Allchin, *Participation in God*, 25.
3. Kimbrough, "*Theosis* in the Writings of Charles Wesley."
4. Russell, *Fellow Workers with God*, 11.

Introduction

resonance of ideas is precisely that and nothing more. It is very much like the example in biblical studies of two twentieth-century scholars: Max Weber and Antonin Causse. The former was the distinguished German sociologist who wrote a phenomenally perceptive book on the birth and emergence of Judaism, *Das antike Judentum*. The latter was a French professor of Old Testament who was greatly influenced by the French sociologists Émile Durkheim and Lucien Lévy-Bruhl and wrote an extremely important volume also on the birth and emergence of Judaism, *Du groupe ethnique à la communité religieuse*. Weber, as a sociologist, wrote a substantive history of Judaism seen through the lens of his sociological method. Causse, as an Old Testament specialist, wrote a history of the emergence of Judaism using the tools of French sociological analysis and sound historical critical method. Though they lived in the same period, one in Germany and the other in France, they never met and apparently did not read each other's works. Even so, they came to many of the same conclusions sociologically and historically.

As in the case of Weber and Causse, whose works stand on their own scholarly integrity and remain of great value in the study of Judaism and biblical studies, it is not absolutely necessary for there to be verification of Charles Wesley's reading of the church fathers in order for the congruencies of thought and resonance of ideas to have value for theology in the East and West. It will be clear in the course of this study, however, that there are other avenues for the intersection of the church fathers and Charles Wesley.

This volume explores Charles Wesley's understanding of participation in the divine nature in the larger context of his prose and poetical compositions and in relation to some of the church fathers.[5] Interestingly, it is often claimed that the concept of deification is an unfamiliar and perhaps offensive idea in Western Christianity,[6] if not sacrilegious. J. Stamoolis maintains

---

5. There are a number of scholars who have traced Orthodox influences in Wesleyan theology. See Outler, *John Wesley*, who avers that Wesley's reading of patristic texts influenced his theology; Maddox, "John Wesley and Eastern Orthodoxy" and *Responsible Grace*, where he sees some similarities between the Wesleyan doctrine of perfection/sanctification and the Orthodox concept of deification; Campbell, *John Wesley and Christian Antiquity*; and Heitzenrater, "John Wesley's Reading of and References to the Early Church Fathers," who does not doubt the presence of patristic influence but claims that "the precise shape of the theological and spiritual genealogy that passed on such a heritage remains fully to be described" (31). See also the annotated bibliography and discussion in my essay "Charles Wesley and a Window to the East," 169–83, and Wakefield, "Charles Wesley's Spirituality and Its Meaning for Today," 79–99.

6. See Archimandrite George, *Theosis*, 10.

that a legalistic approach to justification over against the concept of mystical union integral to Orthodoxy is the "real issue that unites the West theologically [that is, both Catholics and Protestants] and divides it from the East."[7] Daniel Keating prefers a more balanced view when he says, "The doctrine of deification is not the patrimony of the Eastern church alone, or of an eccentricity of certain schools of Western theology. Rather deification concerns the basic economy of God in Christ through the Spirit that is at the patristic root of both the Eastern and Western theological traditions."[8] Nevertheless, the Eastern Church has been the primary harbinger of the doctrine of deification from the patristic era to the present.

Although deification may not have been a dominant concept in Western theology, it is by no means absent. While there has been an ongoing revival of interest in deification in the Eastern Church,[9] there has been a renewed interest as well in the West, particularly among Lutherans,[10] Roman Catholics,[11] Anglicans,[12] and scholars of the Wesleyan tradition.[13] A. M. Allchin has clearly demonstrated in his work *Participation in God: A Forgotten Strand in Anglican Tradition*[14] that the idea of participation unquestionably exists in the theology of Anglican priest Richard Hooker (1554–1600),

---

7. Stamoolis, *Eastern Orthodox Mission Theology Today*, 7–11.

8. Keating, *Deification and Grace*, 5–6.

9. Of particular importance are the following volumes, which are benchmark studies in the renewed and ongoing interest in deification by Orthodox theologians: Meyendorff, *Byzantine Theology*; Stavropoulos, *Partakers of the Divine Nature*; Ware, "Salvation and Theosis in Orthodox Theology"; Mantzaridis, *The Deification of Man*. See also V. Lossky, *The Mystical Theology of the Eastern Church* and *In the Image and Likeness of God*; Gross, *La divinization du chrétien d'après les Pères grecs* (1938), English trans. *The Divinization of the Christian according to the Greek Fathers* (2002); Russell, *The Doctrine of Deification in the Greek Patristic Tradition* and *Fellow Workers with God*.

10. Kärkkäinen, *One with God*; Braaten and Jenson, *Union with Christ*. There has also been exploration of deification in the works of John Calvin, e.g., Mosser, "The Greatest Possible Blessing: Calvin and Deification."

11. Keating, *Deification and Grace* and *The Appropriation of Divine Life in Cyril of Alexandria*.

12. The significant research of Anglican A. M. Allchin is noted further in this paragraph. However, the more recent thorough research of Anglican Paul M. Collins is an important addition to the renewed interest in deification: *Partaking in Divine Nature*. See also Mascall, *Christ, the Christian and the Church*, and Louth, "Manhood into God."

13. McCormick, "Theosis in Chrysostom and Wesley"; Christensen, "Theosis and Sanctification"; Kimbrough, "*Theosis* in the Writings of Charles Wesley." See above, footnote 5.

14. Allchin, *Participation in God*, 24–48.

Introduction

Anglican bishop and scholar Lancelot Andrewes (1555–1626), Anglican priest/poet and one of the founders of the Methodist movement Charles Wesley (1707–88), and Welsh hymn writer and a leader of the Welsh Methodist revival William Williams Pantycelyn (1717–91). In addition, Allchin elucidates the importance of the doctrine of deification among leaders of the Oxford Movement—John Keble[15] (1792–1866), Edward Bouverie Pusey[16] (1800–1882), and John Henry Newman[17] (1801–90).

As regards the origin of patristic influence on Charles Wesley, an interesting suggestion has been made by Geoffrey Wainwright. After commenting on various readings and individuals by way of which John Wesley was introduced to a variety of patristic sources and church fathers prior to and during his stay in the American colonies, Wainwright suggests, "Through the Oxford and Georgia years, the contact between John and Charles was very close, and we may therefore reasonably assume that Charles became familiar with the patristic and Anglican texts by way of John, even if evidence is lacking to show that he did so directly."[18]

There was unquestionably a favorable intellectual environment in the seventeenth- and eighteenth-century English Reformation for the use of the metaphor of deification in Anglican theological thinking.[19] Nevertheless, the concept of deification did not become dominant in Anglican theology or preaching, but its presence among some leading thinkers of the English Reformation unquestionably influenced its appearance in the works of some leaders of eighteenth-century revival movements, such as John and Charles Wesley.

Charles Wesley did not construct a systematic exposition of the concept of participation, but he frequently utilized language that is similar to patristic explications of deification. Even if the patristic influence in this regard is largely through Lancelot Andrewes—as averred by A. M. Allchin[20] and Nicholas Lossky[21]—and through Richard Hooker, one must ask, what

---

15. Ibid., 53.
16. See his *Holy Eucharist a Comfort to the Penitent*.
17. See his *Lectures on Justification*.
18. Wainwright, "Our Elder Brethren Join," 11.
19. See the summary statement on this period by Collins, *Partaking in Divine Nature*, 152–56.
20. Allchin, *Participation in God*.
21. Lossky, "Lancelot Andrewes: A Bridge between Orthodoxy and the Wesley Brothers in the Realm of Prayer." Also Lossky, *Lancelot Andrewes the Preacher (1555–1625): The Origins of the Mystical Theology of the Church of England*.

were the specific influences of Andrewes and Hooker on Charles Wesley? Had Wesley read or was he aware of the following statement in Andrewes' Christmas Day sermon of 1605? "He taking our flesh, and we receiving His Spirit; by His flesh which he took of us receiving His Spirit which he imparteth to us; that, as He by ours became *consors humanae naturae* [partaker of human nature], so we by His might become *consortes Divinae naturae,* 'partakers of the Divine nature.'"[22] Even if specific attestation of Andrewes' influence on Charles Wesley is not always forthcoming, the former's strong averment that we are deified through the Eucharist finds resonance in many of Charles Wesley's hymns for Holy Communion.

It should be noted that Charles Wesley possessed in his personal library *The Works of Richard Hooker . . . in Eight Books of Ecclesiastical Polity*. Most certainly he must have read the following comment of Hooker in Book 1: "although we be men, yet being unto God united we live as it were the life of God."[23] Allchin writes that "Hooker opens up the way for a reaffirmation of the patristic conviction that man can indeed become partaker of the divine nature, but only and always by gift and grace, never by right and nature."[24]

In reading Hooker's *Ecclesiastical Polity* Charles Wesley would have encountered a broad array of the church fathers: St. Irenaeus, St. Athanasius, St. Gregory of Nazianzus, St. Cyprian, St. Jerome, St. Ignatius, St. John Chrysostom, Tertullian, St. Augustine, and St. Ambrose.

He would also have encountered Hooker's reflections on the concept of "participation" in Book 5[25] of *Ecclesiastic Polity* where he wrote, "By this participation, initiated by God, Christians are incorporated into that societie which hath him for theire head and doth make together with him one bodie . . . for which cause by vertue of this mysticall conjunction wee are of him and in him even as though our verie flesh and bones should be made continuate with his."[26]

In this study we ask, How does Charles Wesley's thinking on participation resonate with the thinking of the church fathers, for he indeed emphasizes time and again that followers of Christ are to be "partakers of the life divine"? How do his views converge with or diverge from the church fathers?

22. *Lancelot Andrewes Works.* Sermons (vol. 1: *Sermons of the Nativity*).
23. Hooker, *Ecclesiastical Polity*, I.11.2.
24. Allchin, *Participation in God*, 13.
25. See Booty's excellent "Commentary" on Richard Hooker's Book 5.
26. 56.7; 2:238.30—239.5.

INTRODUCTION

There follow some briefly summarized perspectives on deification of the church fathers to which this discussion will return from time to time. (1) St. Clement of Alexandria (150-215) views deification as assimilation to God as far as possible. (2) Origen (145-254) sees human deification as a possibility, since God has become human in Christ. He makes "participation in the divine" a seminal aspect of his theology. However, deification for him is not instantaneous, but rather a progressive process. (3) St. Ephrem the Syrian (306-73) also adheres to the perspective of progressive deification. (4) St. Gregory of Nazianzus (328-90) prefers the word *deification* and uses the metaphor of polishing a mirror to describe the deification process. (5) St. Gregory of Nyssa (335-99) prefers "participation in God" and sees no limits to the human movement toward perfection and the knowledge of God that can be progressively acquired. Like many others, the transformation for him is gradual. He conceives of three ways of the spiritual journey: the way of light, the way of the cloud, and the way of darkness, the last of which involves "participation." However, "'Deification' is a word he reserves for the operation of Christ in the sacraments."[27] (6) St. Cyril of Alexandria (ca. 376-444) understands deification to be the ultimate goal of human beings. (7) St. Maximus the Confessor's (580-662) view of *theosis* as *perichoresis*, the interpenetration of God and humanity, gives deification a fixed place in Orthodox theology. (8) In the fourteenth century St. Gregory Palamas (1296-1359) developed a distinction between the divine essence and the divine energies and averred that deification transpires by way of participation in the divine energies.[28] His volume *On Divine and Deifying Participation* precipitated ongoing systematic analysis of this doctrine among Orthodox scholars.

While the above summary is much too brief and inadequate to describe the perspectives of those listed, it is important in addressing how Charles Wesley's theology of participation may be evaluated against a background of these earlier views.[29]

---

27. Russell, *Fellow Workers with God*, 130.

28. See Papademetriou, *Introduction to Saint Gregory Palamas*, 27-35, 43-44; Meyendorff, *Study of Gregory Palamas*, 202-27.

29. See Norman Russell's excellent summary of the history of the Orthodox development of the language and concept of theosis/deification in *Fellow Workers with God*, particularly chs. 1-3 (33-91). See also the thorough discussion of Collins in *Partaking in Divine Nature*, especially chs. 3 ("Early Church Witness"), 4 ("The Doctrine of Deification in Orthodoxy"), and 5 ("The 'Architecture' of the Metaphor in the West").

1

Background: Charles Wesley's Theology of Mystery

There have been a few significant studies of Charles Wesley's ideas related to deification, particularly as pertains to his brother John's perspectives and those of some of the early church fathers.[1] Perhaps the most important study is that of A. M. Allchin, *Participation in God: A Forgotten Strand in Anglican Tradition*, in which the author avers that Charles Wesley reflects "an earlier view" of deification than John.[2] Allchin uses Wesley's poetry effectively in his discussion,[3] but as I have noted elsewhere,[4] "'an earlier view' suggests a chronology of theological understanding and development,"[5] which may miss an important aspect of Wesley's view of participation: namely, he understands it within a "theology of mystery" that is not necessarily bound by a chronological development of theological ideas.

Allchin includes in the volume just mentioned a quotation from Nicholas Lossky that is a superb summary of the theology of Lancelot Andrewes, which could also be a description of the theology of Charles Wesley, whose name in brackets is substituted for Andrewes.

> The final goal of spiritual life being union with God, one can say that the theology of [Charles Wesley] is a mystical theology, as

---

1. See Christensen, "*Theosis* and Sanctification: John Wesley's Reformulation of a Patristic Doctrine."

2. Christensen follows Allchin's view in "John Wesley: Christian Perfection as Faith Filled with the Energy of Love."

3. In his well-written chapter, "Deification," in *Christian Spirituality: Essays in Honour of Gordon Rupp*, 33–62, Ben Drewery is not as successful as Allchin in his use of Charles Wesley's poetry. Rather than analyze or carefully study its specific implications for deification, he opts to address almost singularly scriptural holiness.

4. Kimbrough, "*Theosis* in the Writings of Charles Wesley."

5. Ibid., 211.

long as one elucidates the meaning of the word "mystical." It is not a question of an exceptional experience, reserved for a few, in some way outside the traditional ways of theology. On the contrary it is a question of the interiorisation of the revealed Christian mystery, to which [Wesley] calls all baptised. This theology is mystical in the sense that it is not an abstract reflection, but a concrete way of living the mystery in the deepening of the faith through prayer and the renunciation of one's own will. It is a way of the submission of the human to the divine will, which allows the grace of the Holy Spirit to impregnate human nature. For [Wesley] it is altogether clear that this is only possible in fidelity to the given realities of revelation, that is to say in the scriptural and patristic tradition, or in other words in the catholicity of the Church.[6]

In another important study, *The Kingdom of Love and Knowledge: The Encounter between Orthodoxy and the West*, Allchin has shown numerous similarities and some divergences between the theology of St. Symeon the New Theologian and Charles Wesley.

Theology of Mystery

Charles Wesley's views on any aspect of theology should be seen within the context of a theology of mystery. He struggles to find a balance between the desire to know and the realization that one cannot know the Mystery fully. He is overwhelmed by the thought of God's expression of love for all humankind in Christ. After reading Deut 7:7–8, "The LORD did not set his love upon you because ye were more in number than any people, but because the LORD loved you," he penned eight eloquent lines that are the fulcrum of his theological perspective.

> What angel can explain
> The love of God to man,
> The secret cause assign
> Of charity divine?
> Nothing in us could move,
> Deserve, or claim his love:
> *'Tis all a mystery*,
> And must forever be![7]

---

6. Lossky, *Lancelot Andrewes*, 367, quoted in Allchin, *Participation in God*, 22.
7. *Scripture Hymns* 1762, 1:93, Hymn 293. Italics added for emphasis.

Wesley is awestruck by the expression of divine love toward him and all humankind and knows indubitably that no one deserves such love. Furthermore, no one in earth or heaven, no angel, can explain God's charity. It is, and shall always be, a mystery.

In another poem from the same publication, *Scripture Hymns* 1762, he emphasizes yet further the incomprehensibility of God.

1. Shall foolish, weak, short-sighted man
   Beyond archangels go,
The great almighty God explain,
   Or to perfection know?
His attributes divinely soar
   Above the creatures' sight,
And prostrate *Seraphim* adore
   The glorious Infinite.

2. *Jehovah's* everlasting days
   They cannot numbered be,
Incomprehensible the space
   Of thine immensity;
Thy wisdom's depths by reason's line
   In vain we strive to sound,
Or stretch our labouring thought t'assign
   Omnipotence a bound.

3. The brightness of thy glories leaves
   Description far below;
Nor man, nor angel's heart conceives
   How deep thy mercies flow:
Thy love is *most* unsearchable,
   And dazzles all above;
They gaze, but cannot count or tell
   The treasures of thy love![8]

---

8. *Scripture Hymns* 1762, 1:231–32; based on Job 11:7: "Canst thou by searching find out God? canst thou find out the Almighty unto perfection?" Italics added for emphasis, except for proper names.

Background: Charles Wesley's Theology of Mystery

In these lines Wesley produces a cascading description of God's incomprehensibility. Most assuredly finite man is incapable of transcending archangels in order to comprehend God. Divine immensity is inconceivable. Though reason seeks to grasp divine wisdom, it strives in vain. He uses an interesting analogy when he says that not even the heart of angels can grasp the depth of God's mercy. Then comes the crowning comment: "Thy love is *most* unsearchable." This is fascinating because love is the key to Charles Wesley's theology, indeed to his theology of participation. The most comprehensive statement for him in Scripture about God's nature is that "God is love" (1 John 4:8), yet, it is "*most* unsearchable"!

As is claimed by many Eastern theologians,[9] Wesley also affirms that the human experience of God comes through the visitation of the Holy Spirit. It is the means whereby the Word of God is made present and powerful in the lives of humankind. It is the real presence of the divine, which unites us to God in Christ and fulfills the incomprehensible mystery. This yearning for the visitation of the Holy Spirit is found in the following prayer of Charles Wesley.

> The word is unaccomplished still:
> In honour of thy Son,
> Father, *the mystery fulfill*,
> And send the promise down;
> That Spirit of universal grace,
> That Spirit of glory pour,
> And deluge all our ransomed race
> With one eternal shower.[10]

Divine Essence

In another poem in *Scripture Hymns 1762*, Wesley uses language of mystery similar to that of some Orthodox theologians when he speaks of the divine

---

9. For example, St. Seraphim of Sarov: "When the Spirit of God descends upon a man and overshadows him with the fullness of his outpouring, then his soul overflows with a joy not to be described, for the Holy Spirit turns to joy whatever he touches" (*Concerning the Aim of the Christian Life*, 56). See also St. Symeon the New Theologian, *Hymns* 22 and 28, in vol. 2 of Koder, *Hymns*.

10. *Scripture Hymns 1762*, 2:73, Hymn 1333, based on Joel 2:28, "I will pour out my Spirit on all flesh." Italics added for emphasis.

as "essence incomprehensible." St. Maximus the Confessor expressed the idea in this manner: "We do not know God in his essence. We know him rather from the grandeur of his creation and from his providential care for all creatures. For by this means, as if using a mirror, we attain insight into his infinite goodness, wisdom and power."[11]

Charles Wesley also affirms that God is "essence" and hence cannot be fully comprehended. In the following poem one encounters the verb *know*, which is characteristic of his writing for he is deeply concerned with "knowing" God. In responding to Jer 31:34, "They shall all know me," he wrote the following lines:

> *Essence incomprehensible*,
>   Jehovah, who can know,
> Who was, and is, and comes to dwell
>   With all his saints below!
> Then the whole world shall be restored
>   And bow to Jesu's name,
> Filled with the knowledge of the Lord,
>   The infinite I AM.[12]

How can this be? If the incarnation is a reality, does one not "know" God through the incarnate Son, Jesus Christ? That God should so love humankind and express that love through the Word made flesh is for Wesley an incomprehensible mystery. One can know God through the divine act of the incarnation, but God's essence, the otherness of God, is incomprehensible. St. Athanasius averred, "He [God] is outside all things according to his essence, but he is in all things through his acts of power."[13] This is precisely the perspective of Charles Wesley in the poem just quoted.

Wesley's "essence incomprehensible" resonates with words of St. Symeon the New Theologian. "The divine and uncreated superessential nature as transcending the essence of all created things is called super-essence, yet still has an essence and is personal, [though it is] beyond all essence and is conceived as completely incomparable with any created person, for it is wholly uncircumscribed by nature. How can you call what is indescribable

---

11. St. Maximus the Confessor, *On Love*, i. 96.
12. *Scripture Hymns* 1762, 2:33, Hymn 1233. Italics added for emphasis.
13. Athanasius, *On the Incarnation* 17 (Thomson, 174).

a person? Yet what is not a person is nothing—and how is it communicable to me?"[14]

Of course, the distinction between divine essence and divine energies was more sharply delineated by St. Gregory Palamas[15] and defenders of the neo-Palamite school such as Vladimir Lossky[16] and John Meyendorff.[17] Kallistos Ware delineates the two quite lucidly: "Essence signifies the whole God as he is in himself; the energies signify the whole of God as he is in action."[18]

Divine Energy

Charles Wesley also speaks of divine energy.

1. Can these dry bones perceive
     The quickening power of grace,
 Or Christian infidels retrieve
     The life of righteousness?
     All-good, almighty Lord,
     Thou know'st thine own design,
 The virtue of thine own great world,
     The energy divine.

2. Now for thy mercy's sake
     Let thy great word proceed,
 Dispensed by whom thou wilt, to wake
     The spiritually dead;
     Send forth to prophesy
     Thy chosen messenger,
 And thou the gospel-word apply,
     And force the world to hear.[19]

---

14. Hymn 52, quoted in Golitzin, *On the Mystical Life*, 3:134.

15. See Krivocheine, "Essence créée et essence divine dans la théologie spirituelle de S. Syméon le nouveau théologien."

16. Lossky, *The Mystical Theology of the Eastern Church*.

17. Meyendorff, *A Study of Gregory Palamas*.

18. Ware, *Orthodox Way*, 22.

19. Scripture Hymns 1762, 2:51, based on Ezek 37:3–4, "And he said unto me, Son of man, can these bones live? And I answered, O Lord God, thou knowest. Again he said

How is one to interpret Wesley's references to divine essence and divine energy? To be sure, he does not fall prey to the theological view in the West that God is only essence. Even though his language seems to resonate with a Palamite interpretation of God's nature, this may be a coincidence rather than intentional. Unquestionably he speaks of divine essence as incomprehensible and unknowable ("Jehovah, who can know"). Yet, it is the incomprehensible God "Who was, and is, and comes to dwell / With all his saints below!" The unknowable God becomes knowable through the divine act of the incarnation. This is, of course, the Mystery *par excellence.*

Wesley does not elaborate further the meaning of "Essence incomprehensible," though he returns to this idea at times in his poetry. Hence, it is futile to attempt to fit his intended meaning exactly into the Palamite interpretation described by Jeffrey D. Finch.

> The essence or *ousia* of God, Palamas and his followers propose . . . does not properly denote the full, incomprehensible measure of who God is—God's fully actuated, infinite Quiddity, as it were—but refers only to a particular "mode" or dimension of God's being. "The essence is necessarily being, but being is not necessarily essence: this principle," writes Meyendorff, "is the real significance of what is called 'Palamism.'"[20] God transcends God's self, his essence surpassing his being or existence and his being surpassing his essence.[21]

Nevertheless, it is somewhat tempting to see Wesley's views against a Palamite background. He does speak of "the energy divine" as different from the "essence incomprehensible." It is identified with "the quickening power of grace," which would appear to be God's action and knowable, therefore an experience of God beyond the bounds of divine essence. "The energy divine" is also related to "the life of righteousness," which involves active engagement to live a righteous life, and according to God's "own design." It is "the energy divine" which is to carry out the divine design. Therefore, it is through divine energy that participation in the divine nature takes place. Here Wesley's thought seems to be in concert with St. Basil, who says, "We

---

unto me, Prophesy upon these bones, and say unto them, O ye dry bones, hear the word of the LORD." Italics added for emphasis.

20. Meyendorrf, *Study of Gregory Palamas*, 213.
21. Finch, "Neo-Palamism," 237.

Background: Charles Wesley's Theology of Mystery

know the essence through the energy. No one has ever seen the essence of God, but we believe in the essence because we experience the energy."[22]

In stanza 2 of the aforecited poem, Wesley describes further how God's energy is involved in the world. It dispenses God's word to whom God wills; it wakes "the spiritually dead"; it sends forth God's chosen messenger to prophesy and apply the gospel-word. Finally, "the energy divine" forces "the world to hear." Clearly for Wesley the divine energy moves beyond the incomprehensible essence in ways that are recognizable to humankind through God's action.

Though there are distinct similarities, it would be ill-advised to aver that Wesley is speaking of divine essence and divine energy specifically in the sense of the church fathers St. Symeon the New Theologian and St. Gregory Palamas. Nevertheless, his ideas are quite similar. When he takes up the idea of "participation" in God, at no point does he aver that we partake of "the essence incomprehensible." He most certainly affirms that the active engagement of "the energy divine" is knowable. Herewith his ideas are generally in concert with many church fathers and contemporary Orthodox theologians, for God is "at the same time incomprehensible (*akateleptos*) in His essence, and comprehensible by His creatures in His divine energies."[23]

However one may read Charles Wesley's plethora of references to deification in his writings, they must always be viewed against a background of a theology of mystery.

---

22. St. Basil, *Doctrina patrum de incarnatione verbi*, 88–89.
23. Papademetriou, *Introduction to Saint Gregory Palamas*, 44.

2

Prose Sources: Journal and Sermons

First, we shall examine Wesley's comments related to participation in the divine nature in his prose writings.

The Journal

Almost all attempts to explore Charles Wesley's theology of participation begin and end with his poetry. Unquestionably his poetry is the primary reservoir of his articulation of such a theology, and it forms a major part of this study. However, we begin at a different place, namely with his prose writings—journal and sermons.

We commence with quotations of some passages from his journal in which he uses the phrase "participation of the divine nature" to define the meaning of religion.

> Wednesday, June 11 [1740]. Was constrained to bear my testimony for the last time at Blendon. Maxfield accompanied me. I desired to speak with Mrs Delamotte alone. She did not well know how to refuse, and walked with me into the hall. I began, "Three years ago God sent me to call you from the form to the power of godliness. *I told you what true religion was, a new birth, a participation of the divine nature.*[1] The way to this I did not know myself till a year after. Then I showed it to you, preaching Jesus Christ, and faith in his blood.[2]

Charles refers to a conversation that he had with Mrs. Delamotte three years earlier, that is, 1737. There is a brief entry in his *MSJ* for August

---

1. Italics added for emphasis.
2. *MSJ*, 1:265–66.

18, 1737, which states, "Hearing that Mrs Delamotte was now in town, I went to see her. We fell into discourse upon resignation, and she seemed resolved to acquiesce in the will of God, detaining her Isaac from her."[3] Three years later (1740) he records in the *MSJ* a personal conversation with Mrs. Delamotte and defines true religion as "a new birth, a participation of the divine nature." He says that this is what he told her in 1737, though the *MSJ* entry for August 18, 1737, of the earlier encounter does not state this. One can but accept that Wesley is recalling his earlier conversation with Mrs. Delamotte. When he says, "this I did not know myself till a year after," one assumes he is referring to his conversion experience on May 21, 1738.

While one encounters time and again in his poetry the idea of participation in the divine nature, here he specifically defines religion with language that is usually associated with deification. While through the patristic influence by way of Lancelot Andrewes and Richard Hooker, Wesley came into contact with such language, there is yet another source with which he became intimately familiar that used precisely the same language to define religion. *The Life of God in the Soul of Man*, by Henry Scougal (1650–78), sometimes called "Aberdeen's immortal mystic," originally published in 1677, became extremely influential and popular with the Wesley brothers. John published a number of editions of the little book[4] and Charles's gesture of giving a copy to George Whitefield led to a life-transforming experience for the latter. Here is a passage from Scougal's work that Charles Wesley must have known well.

> But certainly religion is quite another thing, and they who are acquainted with it will entertain far different thoughts, and disdain all those shadows and false imitations of it. They know by experience that true religion is a union of the soul with God, *a real participation of the divine nature*, the very image of God drawn upon the soul, or, in the apostle's phrase, "It is Christ formed within us."—Briefly, I know not how the nature of religion can be more fully expressed, than by calling it a Divine Life: and under these terms I shall discourse of it, showing first, how it is called a life; and then, how it is termed divine.[5]

---

3. Ibid., 1:86.

4. No doubt John agreed to some extent with the language of "participation of the divine nature" in Scougal's volume; however, in appropriating the texts of St. Macarius it is interesting that he essentially omitted references to deification. See Campbell, *John Wesley and Christian Antiquity*, x.

5. Scougal, *Life of God*, 30. Italics added for emphasis.

How then is Wesley using the word *participation*? Does he mean a simple dictionary rendering, namely, to share in some way with others? Norman Russell stresses that there is a sense in which *participation* "is used to account for whatever has no being in its own right, whatever is not self-caused: things exist 'by participation' when they depend on something else. They have no identity conceivable entirely in [themselves]."[6] This would appear to be Wesley's intent in his use of the word, for his response has a strong christocentric focus, as he commented to Mrs. Delamotte: "Then I showed it to you, preaching Jesus Christ, and faith in his blood." Clearly the pronoun *it* refers to the phrase "participation of the divine nature." Without knowing Christ there is no such participation. The incarnation is the enabler of true human identity. Here Wesley differs decidedly from Hellenistic philosophy in which divine nature is an implicit aspect of human nature. To the contrary, according to Wesley we are deified because we know Christ.

On another occasion during the same year Wesley defines religion to a group of coal miners as "a participation of the divine nature." The phrase becomes a means of explaining, perhaps to men with little or no education, what some have "experienced" as religion. While one tends to think of such a phrase as part of rather astute theological language for the learned, for Wesley it defines the central meaning of religious experience of every human being. In contrast to his private statement to Mrs. Delamotte, the following *MSJ* comment indicates that this was probably a public statement.

> Tuesday, July 15 [1740]. To the colliers I described, what many of them have experienced, religion, *a participation of the divine nature*. At Bristol I pressed the example of the primitive Christian, Acts 2, and tasted something of their spirit.[7]

Here Wesley's comment indicates that "a participation of the divine nature" is more than a mere definition of religion. It is an experience. He says that this is what many of them, that is, the colliers, have experienced. While participation, as shall be seen in many of his poems or hymns, is unequivocally the result of God's activity, indeed God's gift, it also involves human response—one *partakes* of the divine nature, one *participates* in the divine nature.

Wesley's idea of "participation of the divine nature" is here perhaps close to Gregory of Nyssa's concept of μετουσία Θεοῦ, that is, participation

---

6. See Russell, *Fellow Workers with God*, 127.
7. *MSJ*, 273. Italics added for emphasis.

in God. In his *Catechetical Oration* Gregory describes such participation as a primary purpose of creation.

> Since he was created to take part in divine blessings, man must have a natural affinity with that object in which he has participation (μετουσία). It is just like an eye which, thanks to the luminous rays which nature provides it, is enabled to have communion (κοινωνία) in the light. . . . It is just so with man, who since he was created to enjoy the divine blessings must have some affinity with that in which he has been called to participate.[8]

Just as Gregory sees μετουσία Θεοῦ as a progression during one's life, Wesley views participation in God as a lifelong, ongoing process.

Wesley's linking of creation and participation in the divine is elaborated further in the discussion below of his sermon on Rom 3:23–5.

It is important to note that the uses of the phrase "participation of the divine nature" in *MSJ* are very early in Charles's career as a priest of the Church of England, having been ordained priest in 1735. In 1740, the year of both entries using the phrase "participation of the life divine," he was thirty-two years of age. Throughout his ministry of fifty-three years he holds fast to this concept.

If "true religion," as Wesley says, is "a participation of the divine nature," then deification is the true purpose of existence. In other words, God has created humankind to participate in the divine nature.

The Sermons

In Charles's sermons one encounters language similar to the *MSJ* passages. In the sermon "Romans 3: 23–5" preached on Sunday, July 1, 1739, he says,

> God created man in his own image, after his likeness. He made him perfect, but a little lower than the angels, one in heart and mind with himself, *a real partaker of the divine nature*.[9] But man soon fell from that original dignity. He sinned by eating of the forbidden fruit, and in the day that he ate he spiritually died. The life of his soul, consisting in its union with God (like as the natural life consists in the union of soul and body) his spiritual life, I say, was extinguished. The glory immediately departed from him, and

---

8. *Catechetical Oration* 5, quoted in McGuckin, "Strategic Adaptation of Deification," 104.

9. Italics added for emphasis.

he knew that he was naked; naked of God, stripped of the divine image; a motley mixture of beast and devil.[10]

Human participation in the divine is linked to creation. At creation man is "one in heart and mind" with God and "a *real* partaker of the divine nature." Wesley speaks of this relationship as "the life of [the] soul, consisting in its union with God (like as the natural life consists in the union of soul and body)." But "union with God . . . was extinguished" through the act of disobedience, that is, "eating of the forbidden fruit." This resulted in spiritual death and man was "stripped of the divine image." Thus, throughout Wesley's poetry one encounters his pleas for the restoration of union with God, that is, with God's nature. He clearly affirms in this sermon that at creation before the fall human beings are "partakers of the divine nature." Nevertheless, it is important to emphasize that for Wesley participation is not simply rectification of the fall; it is the fulfillment of creation. This is vividly expressed in stanza 5 of Hymn 16 in his booklet of forty hymns titled *Preparation for Death* (1772).

> Then, *partaker of thy nature*,
>   I fulfill all the will
> Of my new-creator.[11]

Nevertheless, Wesley does see partaking of the divine nature as the foundation of the incarnation, which, as Alexander Golitzin avers, "undoes and reverses the results of the Fall."[12]

In Charles Wesley's most well-known sermon, "Awake, thou that sleepest," based on Eph 5:14, which he preached on Sunday, April 4, 1742, before the university of Oxford, there are two important passages for this discussion. Both are found in the second part of the sermon.

In the first passage he begins by posing the definitive question for human existence: "Art thou 'partaker of the divine nature'?"

---

10. Wesley, *Sermons*, 188. Note: The words "partaker of" are deciphered from the shorthand "pf," which could also be "partner of" or "participant of." However, in the light of the frequency of Charles's use of both the noun *partaker* and *partake* in reference to participation in the divine nature, "partaker of" would appear to be the best choice.

11. *Preparation for Death* 1772, 19, Hymn 16; stanza 5 of a six-stanza hymn. Italics added for emphasis.

12. Golitzin, *On the Mystical Life*, 3:152.

Prose Sources: Journal and Sermons

> 8. *Art thou "partaker of the divine nature"*[13] [cf. 2 Pet 1:4]? "Knowest thou not that Christ is in thee, except thou be reprobate" [cf. 2 Cor 13:5]? Knowest thou that "God dwelleth in thee, and thou in God, by his Spirit which he hath given thee" [cf. 1 John 3:24; 4:12, 13]? Knowest thou not that "thy body is the temple of the Holy Ghost, which thou hast of God" [cf. 1 Cor 6:19]? Hast thou the "witness in thyself" [cf. 1 John 5:10], "the earnest of thine inheritance" [cf. Eph 1:14]? Art thou "sealed by that Spirit of promise unto the day of redemption" [cf. Eph 1:13; 4:30]? Hast thou "received the Holy Ghost" [Acts 19:2]? Or dost thou start at the question, not knowing whether there be any Holy Ghost?[14]

Wesley is here concerned with the inner life of every human being: "Christ is in thee," "God dwelleth in thee, and thou in God," "thy body is the temple of the Holy Ghost," and "the witness is within thyself." The reception and seal of the Holy Ghost are essential (Eph 1:13). All of these things are related to what it means to be a "partaker of the divine nature."

Wesley goes further, however, and once again provides his definition of religion.

> 10. Yet on the authority of God's Word and our own Church I must repeat the question, "Hast thou received the Holy Ghost?" If thou hast not thou art not yet a Christian; for a Christian is a man that is "anointed with the Holy Ghost and with power" [Acts 10:38]. Thou art not yet made a partaker of pure religion and undefiled [Jas 1:27]. Dost thou not know what religion is? That it is participation in the divine nature [cf. 2 Pet 1:4], the life of God in the soul of man:[15] "Christ in thee, the hope of glory" [cf. Col 1:27]; "Christ formed in thy heart" [Gal 4:19], happiness and holiness; heaven begun upon earth; a "kingdom of God within thee" [cf. Luke 17:21], "not meat and drink," no outward thing, "but righteousness, and peace, and joy in the Holy Ghost" [Rom 14:17]; an everlasting kingdom brought into thy soul, a "peace of God that passeth all understanding" [Phil 4:7], a "joy unspeakable and full of glory" [cf. 1 Pet 1:8]?[16]

---

13. Italics added for emphasis.
14. Wesley, *Sermons*, 218.
15. This is the precise wording of the title of Scougal's book, *The Life of God in the Soul of Man*.
16. Wesley, *Sermons*, 218.

Participation in the divine nature has to do with the indwelling Trinity: "the life of God in the soul of man," "Christ formed in thy heart," and reception of the Holy Ghost—Wesley asks, "Hast Thou received the Holy Ghost?" Thus, the Trinity forms a "kingdom of God within thee." This is what religion is—participation in the divine nature in all of these dimensions. While Wesley does not say that the Holy Ghost is the deifier, as does St. Cyril of Jerusalem in *Catecheses ad illuminandos*,[17] he would appear very close to that claim.

One additional sermon, "The One Thing Needful," which was actually authored by his brother John and was preached by Charles at least six times (perhaps more than that, according to *MSJ*), is important for this discussion. It states explicitly that we are to be partakers of the divine nature.

> III. 3. Be we then continually jealous over our souls, that there be no mixture in our intention. *Be it our one view in all our thoughts, and words, and works, to be partakers of the divine nature*, to regain the highest measure we can of that faith which works by love, and makes us become one spirit with God.[18]

Wesley wishes to remove all doubt that anything could be more significant than participation in the divine nature. It is the most important thing in human existence. It is to be the all-consuming singular perspective for "all our thoughts, words, and works, to be partakers of the divine nature." While one encounters in his poetry the plea "make *me* divine," here he speaks unquestionably in the inclusive plural: "*our* one view," "*our* thoughts, and words, and works," have one purpose—to be "*partakers* of the divine nature." The importance of inclusivity will be significant in the later discussion of Wesley's ecclesial view of participation.

In the remaining chapters of this volume we shall explore a number of dimensions of Charles Wesley's theology of participation in the divine nature. It is incarnational, Trinitarian, sacramental, and ecclesial. Before addressing these dimensions and others, a brief look at Wesley's vocabulary of participation will be useful.

---

17. *Catecheses ad illuminandos* 4.16 (NPNF² 7:23).
18. Wesley, *Sermons*, 367; italics added for emphasis.

Prose Sources: Journal and Sermons

Charles Wesley's Vocabulary of Participation

As already noted the verb *partake* and the noun *partaker*(s) are essential to Wesley's vocabulary. To "partake of" God's nature suggests that one joins in the activity of uniting with God. To "partake of" can mean to be characterized by a quality or to eat or drink as at the Lord's Table. The words *partake* and *partaker*(s) are two of the most prevalently used words by Wesley in expressions pertaining to participation in the divine nature. Here are some examples:

>Till of thy nature I partake
>That I thy nature might partake
>That we might partake the nature divine
>Thy nature we partake
>Partaker(s) of his nature pure
>Partakers of his nature makes
>All who partake of Christ, / Partake the nature properly divine
>And when thy nature I partake
>Partaker of thy nature make
>Partake the nature of my Head

There are many other verbs Wesley uses to express the concept of deification:

>*Change* my nature into thine
>Thy nature *share*
>May we all thy nature *share*
>*Transform* my nature into thine
>*Impress* thy nature on my heart
>Let every soul thy nature *know*
>Thy nature *make known*
>Thy nature to thy church *made known*
>*Make* thy nature known
>And *make* me all divine
>Thy nature with our natures *joined*
>Thy nature doth itself *impart*
>Thy nature to my soul *impart*
>Thy nature I long to *put on*
>His sinless nature to *impart*
>But first *impart* thy nature

Fix thy nature in my heart
And *plant* thy nature in my heart
Fill us with the life divine
Impregnated with life divine

This by no means exhausts Charles Wesley's vocabulary for participation in the divine nature, but one immediately sees from these examples how important they are for this aspect of his theology.

3

The Life Divine and Participation in the Divine Nature

THE FIRST STEP TOWARD an in-depth examination of Wesley's language for participation is to explore what he means by the term "life divine," one of the most prolific expressions in his poetry, which is essentially an equivalent for the "divine nature."

The Source

There is but one source of life divine, the Holy Trinity. It is the integrated activity of the Trinity "to quicken all below," that is, to give life to everyone. Indeed, "each Person of the Three" is the breath of life and possesses the quickening power: the Father imparts power that we feel, the Son exerts the same power, and the Spirit infuses us with grace. Thus, says Wesley, "the whole Trinity concurs" to raise from the dead. In other words, the Trinity enables the resurrected life.

> 1. *Fountain of life divine*
> The Three in One we know,
> The Father, Son, and Spirit join
> To quicken all below;
> Each Person of the Three
> The breath of lives inspires;
> And then we rise our God to see,
> And do what he requires.

2. Spiritual life t' impart
>   The Father's power we feel;
> The Son doth the same power exert
>   And quickens whom he will:
>   The quick'ning Spirit stirs
>   Infusing his own grace;
> And the whole Trinity concurs,
>   Me from the dead to raise.[1]

In another poem from *Trinity Hymns* 1767 Wesley stresses that the unknown triune God takes possession of us. We are sealed as a temple of the Lord and filled with life divine. He begins the poem by emphasizing that he is fixed on the "Athanasian mound." His vantage point for grasping the Holy Trinity is that of Athanasius. He could well be referring to the Athanasian Creed, the first creedal statement in which the equality of three persons of the Trinity was specifically affirmed. He knew it well, for the 1662 BCP required its occasional use in the course of the liturgical year. Nevertheless, he says he requires yet firmer ground. The firmer ground of which he speaks is the inner experience of the Trinity: "I want to *feel* my soul renewed / In the similitude of God." He wants "the whole mysterious Trinity" to inhabit his heart so that he is filled "with all the life divine."

> 1. Thee, great tremendous Deity
>   Whom Three in One, and One in Three
>   I to the world proclaim,
>   Inspire with purity and peace,
>   And add me to thy witnesses
>   By telling me thy name.
>
> 2. Fixed on the Athanasian mound,
>   I still require a firmer ground
>   My sinking faith to bear:
>   I want to feel my soul renewed
>   In the similitude of God,
>   Jehovah's character.

---

1. *Trinity Hymns* 1767, 80, Hymn 125, based on the following passages of Scripture: "The father raiseth up the dead and quickeneth them; even so the Son quickeneth whom he will" (John 5:21), and "It is the Spirit that quickeneth" (John 6:63). Italics added for emphasis.

> 5. Furnished with intellectual light,
> In vain I speak of thee aright,
> While unrevealed thou art:
> Thou only can suffice for me,
> The whole mysterious Trinity
> Inhabiting my heart.
>
> 6. Come then, thou Tri-une God unknown,
> Take full possession of thine own,
> And keep me ever thine,
> An heir of bliss, for glory sealed,
> *A temple of the Lord, and filled*
> *With all the life divine.*²

Here Charles "prays that he might not just proclaim right doctrines but may also live them, discovering the life of God dwelling in his own life."³ He is also struggling in this prayer with intellectual assent to doctrines and the need of inner purity.

The incarnation makes possible knowledge of life divine specifically through God's revelation in Jesus; therefore, Wesley stresses that Jesus is the means whereby life divine is revealed to all. It does not exist apart from him. He is "the well of life divine."

> My soul, a dry and barren place,
> Gasps for the cooling streams of grace;
> O might they thro' the desert roll
> Refreshment to my gasping soul!
> Jesus, I thirst for thee, not thine,
> *I want the well of life divine;*
> *The well of life divine thou art,*
> Spring up eternal in my heart.⁴

---

2. Ibid., 102-3, Hymn 19:1, 2, 5, 6; stanzas 1, 2, 5, 6 of a six-stanza hymn. Italics added for emphasis.

3. Allchin, "Trinity in the Teaching of Charles Wesley," 77-78.

4. *Scripture Hymns* 1762, 1:328–29, Hymn 1018, based on Isa 32:2, "As rivers of water in a dry place." Italics added for emphasis.

Partakers of the Life Divine

The Unspeakable Gift

Life divine cannot be earned; it is a gift that enables one to be a new creation affirmed by faith. Wesley prays,

> The gift unspeakable impart,
>   Command the light of faith to shine,
> To shine in my dark drooping heart,
>   *And fill me with the life divine;*
> Now bid the new creation be,
> O God, let there be faith in me.[5]

How does one receive the gift of life divine? It is made possible by the Holy Spirit, as Wesley makes explicit in Hymn 3 of *Pentecost Hymns* 1746.

> 1.   Eternal Spirit, come
>   Into thy meanest home,
>   From thine high and holy place
>   Where thou dost in glory reign,
>   Stoop in condescending grace,
>   Stoop to the poor heart of man.
>
> 2.   For thee our hearts we lift
>   *And wait the heavenly gift:*
>   *Giver, Lord of life divine,*
>   To our dying souls appear,
>   Grant the grace for which we pine,
>   Give thyself the Comforter.
>
> 3.   No gift or comfort we
>   Would have distinct from thee,
>   Spirit, principle of grace,
>   Sum of our desires thou art,
>   Fill us with thy holiness,
>   Breathe thyself into our heart.

---

5. *Redemption Hymns* 1747, 19, Hymn 14:3; stanza 3 of a five-stanza hymn. Italics added for emphasis.

4.　　　　Our ruined souls repair,
　　　　　　And fix thy mansion there,
　　Claim us for thy constant shrine,
　　　　All thy glorious self reveal,
　Life, and power, and love divine,
　　　God in us forever dwell.[6]

The gift of life divine is an act of grace received in the human heart. Wesley speaks in the first three stanzas of the activity of grace: "condescending grace" (stanza 1), "grant the grace" (stanza 2), and "Spirit, principle of grace" (stanza 3). Life divine is the gift of the Holy Spirit ("give thyself the Comforter") and results in one's inner transformation. One is indwelled by God's Spirit. It breathes itself into our hearts and fills us with holiness. The fall is reversed as our ruined souls are repaired and we are claimed for God's dwelling. To all who experience this inner revelation, God gives "life, and power, and love divine," because "God in us forever dwell[s]." We have divine life, divine power, and divine love within. This is the new creation of which Wesley speaks.

Knowledge

The Holy Spirit not only enables sharing in the life divine, it enables knowledge of the Godhead. The Spirit comes to dwell within us "to make the depths of Godhead known" and to sanctify us. It would be a gross error to assume that human knowledge is simply ignored in the gift of the Spirit. To the contrary, the human mind is engaged through the gift. "To make the depths of Godhead known" is not merely an abstract idea or a divine knowledge that bypasses human knowledge.

　　Send us the Spirit of thy Son,
　　To make the depths of Godhead known,
　　　To make us share the life divine;
　　Send him the sprinkled blood t' apply,
　　Send him, our souls to sanctify,
　　　And show, and seal us ever thine.[7]

---

6. *Pentecost Hymns* 1746, 5–6, Hymn 3. Italics added for emphasis.
7. Ibid., 4, Hymn 1:6; stanza 6 of an eight-stanza hymn. Italics added for emphasis.

Partakers of the Life Divine

In Hymn 15 of *Nativity Hymns 1745* Wesley combines vital elements of the life divine and its effect on one's existence.

> I long thy coming to confess
> The mystic power of godliness,
> *The life divine to prove,*
> *The fullness of thy life to know,*
> Redeemed from all my sin below,
> And perfected in love.[8]

(1) He longs for faith in "the mystic power of godliness" revealed in the incarnation. There is a mystic power beyond human intellect that enables one to grasp spiritual truths and through contemplation and self-surrender to be unified with God. (2) At the same time human intellect is not demeaned, for in living the life divine one seeks "the fullness of thy life [the divine life] to know." (3) This engages the human mind. It involves the recognition that one has been redeemed from sin and leads toward perfection in love. (4) The journey toward perfection in love is one that involves being claimed by God's mystic power and the intellectual recognition of God's action.

In stanza 4 of the following hymn from the *Pentecost Hymns 1746* Wesley makes clear that the Spirit of wisdom opens our ears to hear and our eyes to perceive the knowledge imparted by the Spirit of wisdom that is eternal: it "shall never die."

> 1. Spirit of power, 'tis thine alone
> To finish what thyself begun,
> And crown thy work with full success,
> To them that groan beneath their sin,
> Thou bring'st the sweet refreshment in,
> The everlasting righteousness.
>
> 2. Thou dost by thine almighty grace
> Again the abject sinner raise,
> Again our fleshly souls refine,
> Spirit of spirit born, we love,
> And only seek the things above,
> *And live on earth the life divine.*

---

8. *Nativity Hymns 1745*, 20, Hymn 15:6; stanza 6 of an eight-stanza hymn. Italics added for emphasis.

3. Thou dost the vital seed infuse,
    Thou dost the creature new produce
        In all its glorious parts complete,
    The subjects of thy kingdom here
    Thou makest, e'er the judge appear,
        For all thy heavenly kingdom meet.

4. Thou that revealing Spirit art
    Who dost the hearing ear impart,
        The clear illuminated sight,
    Spirit of wisdom from on high,
    Of knowledge that shall never die,
        *Of holy, true, eternal light.*⁹

Live the Life Divine

Something else of vital importance in the previous hymn is the last line of stanza 2, "And live on earth the life divine." Life divine is not an abstract spiritualized idea; it is a reality to be lived. It consumes one's every thought, emotion, and action. This means it must also be inherently pragmatic, for it must apply to all aspects of daily life. So pragmatic is the practice of life divine that one's thoughts at waking and lying down are filled with its reflection. This is what Wesley writes as a hymn for believers "At Lying Down":

7. *Let me of thy life partake;*
    Thy own holiness impart:
    O that I might sweetly wake
        With my Saviour in my heart!
    O that I might know thee mine,
        O that I might thee receive,
    Only live the life divine,
        Only to thy glory live!¹⁰

---

9. *Pentecost Hymns* 1746, 33–34, Hymn 30:1–4; stanzas 1–4 of an eight-stanza hymn. Italics added for emphasis.

10. *HSP* 1749, 1:206, Hymn 6:7 of [Hymns for Believers] "At Lying Down"; stanza 7 an eight-stanza hymn. Italics added for emphasis.

Wesley packs so much into these eight-lines to be prayed before sleeping. (1) Let me partake the life divine. (2) Impart to me divine holiness. (3) Let me wake with Christ in my heart, that "I might know" and receive God intimately. (4) Let me "only live the life divine" and to God's glory. Here in these few lines one finds the essence of deification, at least in Wesley's language. It is the life divine lived each day, every hour of the day.

Wesley reiterates the importance of living the life divine in responding to John 1:12, "And as many as received him, to them gave he power to become the sons of God, even to them that believe on his name," with these lines:

> 2. We yield to be redeemed from sin,
> *The life divine to live,*
> Open our hearts to take thee in;
> And all thy grace receive.
> Thee we receive as God and man,
> Both in one person joined,
> To finish the redeeming plan,
> To rescue all mankind.[11]

Evidence of Life Divine

While life divine unquestionably involves one's inner transformation through the indwelling of the Holy Trinity and with Christ formed in one's heart, there is also external evidence of life divine. While we shall address aspects of the evidence of participation in the divine nature in more detail later in this volume, here we shall note instances in which Wesley relates the external evidence specifically to "life divine." Below is the last stanza (the seventh) of a poem titled "Welcome to the Cross," published in *HSP* 1742.

---

11. Ibid., 2:181, Hymn 28:2; stanza 2 of a thirteen-stanza hymn titled [Hymns for Those that Wait for Redemption]. Italics added for emphasis.

7. Then[12] let me lay my burthen down
>   In sweet forgetfulness of care,
> The cross shall bring me to the crown,
>   The dead thy praises shall declare,
> When all renewed in love I shine,
> *Partaker of the life divine.*[13]

In the earlier stanzas of the poem Wesley laments the earthly appetites and passions that could enter his soul and destroy his will. In the spirit of St. Paul's comment "I die daily" (1 Cor 15:31), in the first two lines of stanza 1 he says, "All hail the Saviour's hallowed cross, / By which I daily die within." He anticipates the time "when all renewed in love I shine, / Partaker of the life divine." Radiant love is evidence of deification, namely, that one is a partaker of the life divine.

If the previous lines of poetry might be considered an anticipation of life beyond death, in the same volume, *HSP* 1742, Wesley connects the restoration of the life divine with the restoration and illumination of God's image and the present possibility that one will refrain from sin.

> *I trust, that to the life divine*
>   Thou wilt my soul restore,
> And I shall in thine image shine,
>   And I shall sin no more.[14]

How does one know who is filled with life divine? In writing of the remnant of the faithful in Sardis (see Rev 3:1–2), Wesley underscores that those who triumph in the fight of faith as partakers of the life divine will shine in the image of God and be prepared for heaven. Their appearance is changed.

---

12. Originally "there" but changed in errata and subsequent editions.

13. *HSP* 1742, 46; stanza 7 of a seven-stanza hymn titled "A Welcome to the Cross." Italics added for emphasis.

14. Ibid., 229; stanza 4 of a ten-stanza hymn based on Rom 3:4, "Let God be true and every man a liar." Italics added for emphasis.

11. *Partakers of the life divine,*
>   Who in the fight of faith o'ercome,
> *They all shall in thine*[15] *image shine,*
>   Made ready for their heavenly home.[16]

Wesley is certain that those who are faithful and patient, who endure the fires of persecution, showing they are sealed by the Spirit with pure hearts, are "Partakers of true holiness, / And filled with all the life divine." Remembering the trials and sufferings of those in Thessalonica and the words of 2 Thess 1:4, "We glory in you, for your patience and faith in all your persecutions and tribulations that ye endure," Wesley wrote,

> 1. No room for glorying in their grace,
>   No cause of thankfulness have we
> For those who faith in words profess,
>   'Till faith's undoubted proofs we see:
> But if they see th' invisible,
>   With patience they the fire endure,
> And thus express the Spirit's seal,
>   And witness thus, their hearts are pure.
>
> 2. These are the followers of their Lord,
>   Who suffer in their Master's cause,
> And never speak one boasting word,
>   And only glory in his cross,
> A pattern to believers these
>   As stars throughout the churches shine,
> *Partakers of true holiness,*
>   *And filled with all the life divine.*[17]

Patient endurance of persecution, showing one is sealed by the Spirit in faith, is the undoubted proof of those who are "partakers of true holiness,

---

15. Original "thy" changed to "thine" from the second edition onward. Italics added for emphasis.

16. *HSP* 1742, 293; stanza 11 of a fourteen-stanza hymn based on Rev 3:1–2, "And unto the angel of the church in Sardis write; These things saith he that hath the seven Spirits of God, and the seven stars; I know thy works, that thou hast a name that thou livest, and art dead. Be watchful, and strengthen the things which remain, that are ready to die: for I have not found thy works perfect before God." Italics added for emphasis.

17. *Scripture Hymns* 1762, 2:327, Hymn 640.

The Life Divine and Participation in the Divine Nature

/ And filled with all the life divine." They have seen the invisible and have silently endured, glorying only in the cross of Christ. They are so filled with life divine that they "as stars throughout the churches shine."

What does Wesley mean by the words "But if they see th' invisible"? We find the answer in another hymn to the Holy Trinity.

1. The witnesses in heaven adored,
   The Father, Holy Ghost, and Word,
   One God with all his church we own,
   In Persons Three for ever One.

2. But 'till our souls are born again,
   We to the truth assent in vain,
   By notions right ourselves deceive,
   And only fancy we believe.

3. The Tri-une God we cannot know,
   Unless he doth the faith bestow,
   Faith which removes our mountain-load,
   And brings us to a pard'ning God:

4. Sure evidence of things unseen,
   Which swallows up the gulf between,
   The light of life divine imparts,
   And forms Jehovah in our hearts.

5. O that we all might thus believe,
   The truth in humble love receive,
   Author of faith our Saviour find
   In God the Father of mankind;

6. In both the Holy Spirit know
   (Who doth where'er he listeth blow)
   And the whole Trinity receive
   For ever in our hearts to live![18]

---

18. *Trinity Hymns* 1767, 101–2, Hymn 18. Italics added for emphasis.

Stanza 4 helps us understand what Wesley means by seeing the invisible. He says there is "Sure evidence of things unseen," which swallows "the gulf between," that is, the seen and the unseen, because life divine imparts light and "forms Jehovah in our hearts." Such an experience means that we find the truth in humble love, which transpires when we receive "the whole Trinity" to live "for ever in our hearts."

4

The Incarnation and Participation in the Divine Nature

The incarnation is the source of "true divinity." "Without the doctrine of our deification by grace," avers A. M. Allchin, "the doctrine of the incarnation in the end loses its meaning and finality."[1] Participation in the divine nature is realized in the reality and experience of the incarnation, and Wesley understands its realization in the context of "the mystery." "The incarnation of the Logos and the Theosis of man are the great mystery of our faith and theology."[2]

> When he did our flesh assume
>   That everlasting Man,
> Mary held him in her womb
>   Whom heaven could not contain!
> Who the mystery can believe?
> *Incomprehensible thou art*;
>   Yet we still by faith conceive,
>   And bear thee in our heart.[3]

In Wesley's *Nativity Hymns* 1745 one finds some of his most enlightening statements on participation and the incarnation. Indeed, some of his most eloquent comments are found in the fifth hymn of this collection: stanzas 1, 5, and 6. Of this hymn Gordon S. Wakefield writes, "There is

---

1. Allchin, *Participation in God*, 6.
2. Archimandrite George, *Theosis*, 32.
3. *Scripture Hymns* 1762, 2:32, Hymn 1231, based on Jer 31:22, "A woman shall compass a man." Italics added for emphasis.

also the hymn on the Incarnation, with its line, paralleled in Herbert and elsewhere in contemporary Christian writings, 'Our God contracted to a span,' a hymn in which is also found the Orthodox doctrine of theosis or deification, or, perhaps better, 'participation in God.'"[4]

> 1. Let earth and heaven combine,
>   Angels and men agree
> To praise in songs divine
>   Th' Incarnate Deity,
> Our God contracted to a span,
> *Incomprehensibly* made man.
>
> 5. He deigns in flesh t'appear,
>   Widest extremes to join,
> To bring our vileness near
>   *And make us all divine:*
> And we the life of God shall know,
> For God is manifest below.
>
> 6. Made perfect first in love,
>   And sanctified by grace,
> We shall from earth remove,
>   And see his glorious face:
> His love shall then be fully showed,
> And man shall all be lost in God.[5]

Stanza 5 emphasizes that a primary purpose of the incarnation is to "make us all divine." Here Wesley's words resonate with St. Athanasius in *De Incarnatione*: "He [God] became human that we might become God; and he revealed himself through a body that we might receive an idea of the invisible Father."[6] These lines resonate as well with two lines from one of the Nativity Hymns of Ephrem the Syrian.

---

4. Wakefield, "Charles Wesley's Spirituality," 3.

5. *Nativity Hymns* 1745, 7–8, Hymn 5:1, 5, 6; three stanzas of a six-stanza hymn. Italics added for emphasis.

6. *De Incarnatione*, 54.

The Incarnation and Participation

> Today the Deity imprinted itself on humanity,
> So that humanity might also be cut into the seal of Deity.[7]

Like the Saint from Nisibis, Wesley shapes in poetical language a lyrical theology, which lends itself to song better than to prose theological discourse. One sings the vision of deification and of a mystical union in which one is "lost in God." Wesley is unquestionably in concert with the Eastern Church in emphasizing the mystical union with God through participation in the divine nature. He does not express the idea of salvation solely in juridical categories.

What Wesley says about participation in stanza 5 is also put similarly by St. Maximus the Confessor: "He deigned in his kindness that we be one and the same with him . . . by joining and knitting us closely together with himself in spirit and leading us to the measure of the spiritual maturity which springs from his own fullness."[8]

One cannot miss Wesley's point in the above poem that participation in the divine nature is the most vital dimension of God entering history in Christ. As Vladimir Kharlamov states, "Deification of a human being is the other side of the incarnation."[9] Therefore, taking part in the liturgical celebration of the incarnation is vital to the church. Dimitar Kirov appropriately accents its importance as follows:

> Taking part in this celebration, one mystically breaks the walls of space and time and enjoys the moment of the uniting of heaven and earth. The light from the star, which guided the Magi, now shines in the very being of believers, of the partakers in this mystery, in worship and gives them more than rational knowledge. The Son of God, who dwells in eternity, through the incarnation and birth enters the time and space of history. Through him, human beings enter eternity. This is one of the main truths, which this fest of the Nativity conveys. God enters humankind, and humankind may enter God (*theosis*).[10]

In the incarnation God takes on human nature and makes real the possibility of the indwelling of the divine nature.

---

7. Ephrem, *Ephrem the Syrian: Hymns*, 1:99 (McVey 74).

8. Letter 2 to John the Cubicularius, 401C, quoted in Louth, *Maximus the Confessor*, 90.

9. Kharlamov, "Rhetorical Application of *Theosis*," 121.

10. Kirov, "Mysticism of Light," 97.

> Being of beings, make
> *In me thy nature known,*
> Who didst thyself my nature take
> In thine incarnate Son;
> Thy majesty display,
> Thy name on me impress,
> And what I am, my soul shall say,
> I am by Jesu's grace.[11]

In Wesley's view there is an amazing reciprocity in the divine and human natures expressed in the above poem. Just as we are to be "partakers of the life divine," God *takes* our nature in the "incarnate Son." Wesley does not mean simply in general terms that God has taken on human nature in the incarnation, for he says, "Who didst thyself *my* nature take"!

Vladimir Kharlamov emphasizes an important aspect of Athanasius' methodology with which Charles Wesley, perhaps unknowingly, concurs: he "makes a distinction between the object of participation and the subject that participates. The subject that participates does not become equal or identical with the object of participation. Thus we are like God, but not identical with God."[12]

The purpose of the incarnation is inseparable from partaking of the divine nature, as Charles Wesley's eloquent theo-poetic language expresses in Hymn 8 of *Nativity Hymns* 1745, and as Bishop Kallistos Ware says, "God's incarnation opens the way to man's deification."[13]

> 5. Made flesh for our sake,
>   *That we might partake*
>   *The Nature Divine,*
>   And again in his image, his holiness shine.
>
> 8. And while we are here
>   Our King shall appear,
>   His Spirit impart,
>   And form his full image of love in our heart.[14]

---

11. *Scripture Hymns* 1762, 1:36, Hymn 109, based on Exod 3:14, "I AM THAT I AM." Italics added for emphasis.

12. Kharlamov, "Rhetorical Application of *Theosis*," 122.

13. Ware, *Orthodox Way*, 74.

14. *Nativity Hymns* 1745, 12, Hymn 8:5, 8; stanzas 5 and 8 of an eight-stanza hymn.

The Incarnation and Participation

The incarnation precipitates the yearning for God's nature to be incarnated within human hearts. Charles Wesley expresses this yearning in unsurpassed poetical diction in the following words of Hymn 15 in *Nativity Hymns* 1745 (stanza 4):

> 4. Didst thou not in thy Person join
> *The natures human and divine,*
>   That God and man might be
> Henceforth inseparably One?
> Haste then, and *make thy nature known,*
>   Incarnated in me.[15]

What stronger statement for participation in the divine nature can there be than this? The answer to Wesley's question is an affirmative one: yes, in the incarnation God joins human and divine natures, "That God and man might be / Henceforth inseparably One." The ultimate purpose of the incarnation and of human existence is the inseparable unity of God and humankind. The opening couplet of stanza 7 of this hymn once again underscores participation as the revelation within mortals of the divine Mystery.

> O Christ, my hope, make known in me
> The great, the glorious Mystery.[16]

Wesley expands this language in *Resurrection Hymns* 1746 when he speaks of God's "mystic incarnation." He is responding to a passage from the Great Litany, which he quotes immediately prior to the poem:

> By the mystery of thy holy incarnation; by thy holy nativity and circumcision; by the baptism, fasting, and temptation; by thine agony, and bloody sweat; by thy cross and passion; by thy precious death and burial; by thy glorious resurrection and ascension; and by the coming of the Holy Ghost, good Lord, deliver us.

> Jesus, show us thy salvation,
>   (In thy strength we strive with thee)
> By thy *mystic incarnation,*
>   By thy pure nativity,

Italics added for emphasis.
15. Ibid., 19, Hymn 15:4; stanza 4 of an eight-stanza hymn. Italics added for emphasis.
16. Ibid., 20, Hymn 15:7, lines 1–2.

> Save us thou, our new-Creator,
> > Into all our souls impart,
> Thy divine unsinning nature,
> > Form thyself within our heart.[17]

The stanza culminates with Wesley's prayer for the internationalization of God's nature: "Form thyself within our heart."

Through the incarnation he emphasizes the divine initiative in the process of participation in God's nature; he writes,

> The Creator of all
> To repair our sad fall,
> From his heaven stoops down,
> *Lays hold of our nature*, and joins to his own.[18]

He sees the incarnation as a "repair of our sad fall" through God's initiative to unite the divine and human natures into one.

In stanza 4 of the same poem Wesley interjects the idea of "sinless perfection" in connection with "knowing" God's nature.

> And shall we not hope,
> After God to wake up,
> *His nature to know?*
> *His nature is sinless perfection below.*

Only in union with God's nature, in knowing God's nature, is sinless perfection possible. It is not a human achievement, but rather a divine gift. Yet, it is a mutual experience, as he notes in the last line of the poem: "Apprehended of God let us God apprehend."

These are Charles Wesley's views in 1745, when he published *Nativity Hymns* 1745. When he published *Scripture Hymns* 1762, his views had not changed. He wrote,

> *Thy nature doth itself impart*
> To every humble, longing heart.[19]

---

17. *Resurrection Hymns* 1746, 10, Hymn 7:1; stanza 1 of a nine-stanza hymn. Italics added for emphasis.

18. *Nativity Hymns* 1745, 18, Hymn 14:2, 4; stanzas 2 and 4 of a five-stanza hymn. Italics added for emphasis

19. *Scripture Hymns* 1762, 1:279, Hymn 882:2; the first two lines of stanza 2 of a two-stanza hymn. Italics added for emphasis.

The Incarnation and Participation

He stresses that God in Christ has bestowed on humankind "the image of the living God, / His nature, and his mind."

> The Morning Star, that glittering bright,
>   Shines to the perfect day,
> The Sun of Righteousness, the light,
>   The life, the truth, the way;
> The image of the living God,
>   *His nature, and his mind,*
> Himself he hath on us bestowed,
>   And all in Christ we find.[20]

In an unusual poetic structure Wesley creates "A Dialogue of Angels and Men" in which one of the responses of the "Men" affirms an interesting equation of the incarnation:

> A: As gods we did in glory shine,
>   Before the world began.
> M: *Our nature too becomes divine,*
>   And God himself is man.[21]

Wesley here affirms what was said long ago by Athanasius of Alexandria in his treatise *De Incarnatione*: "God was made man that we might be made God,"[22] which has become commonly known as the "exchange formula." One of the earliest examples of this mode of expression is found in the writings of Irenaeus: "For it was for this end the Word of God was made man, and He who was the Son of God became the Son of man, that man, having been taken into the Word, and receiving the adoption, might become the son of God."[23] Such a perspective became widely supported by the Cappadocians St. Gregory of Nazianzus and St. Gregory of Nyssa, and by St. John Chrysostom, St. Ephrem the Syrian, St. Maximus the Confessor, St. John of Damascus, and St. Symeon the New Theologian.[24]

---

20. *Redemption Hymns* 1747, 24, Hymn 17:9; stanza 9 of a nine-stanza hymn. Italics added for emphasis.

21. *HSP* 1742, 172–73; stanza 3 of a nine-stanza poem. Italics added for emphasis

22. *De Incarnatione* 54.3.

23. *Adversus Haereses* 3.19.1.

24. Keating also finds resonances of the exchange formula in the West: e.g., Hilary of Poitiers, Ambrose of Milan, Augustine, Thomas Aquinas, Martin Luther, and John Calvin (*Deification and Grace*, 13–15).

We have noted at the outset of this study that it is important to understand Charles Wesley's theology of participation in the divine nature within the context of mystery. The union with God is for him a mystical union.

Not only in the birth of Christ does one participate in the divine nature but in and through his resurrection, both being vital moments of the incarnation. In Hymn 5 of Wesley's *Resurrection Hymns* 1746 he expresses quite emphatically that followers of Christ bear in themselves God's nature into eternity. This is yet another dimension of participation in Charles Wesley's theology, namely, that mortals embody the nature of God in the present and in the future.

> 5. Ah! Lord, if thou indeed art ours,
>   If thou for us hast burst the tomb,
> Visit us with thy quickening powers,
>   Come to thy mournful followers, come,
> Thyself to thy weak members join,
> *And fill us with the Life Divine.*
>
> 10. Ought not the members all to pass
>   The way their Head has passed before?
> Thro' sufferings perfected he was,
>   The garment dipped in blood he wore,
> That we with him might die, and rise,
> And *bear his nature* to the skies![25]

In the incarnation God links the natures, human and divine, and through the resurrection of Christ enables mortals to embody, or bear the divine nature from now and into eternity.

This discussion of Charles Wesley's view of participation in the divine nature in relationship to the incarnation makes clear that one may approach his understanding of "being made divine" only in the context of the ultimate Mystery, which cannot be fully comprehended. Yet, it is the incarnation that makes possible the reality and experience of partaking of the divine nature. It is God's gift of and through the incarnation that claims us. How is one's nature transformed into the divine? This remains a mystery, but the faithful are sustained in the Eucharist by God, who links human and divine natures through the elements of bread and wine, and thus as Charles Wesley says, "makes divine."

---

25. *Resurrection Hymns* 1746, 7, 8, Hymn 5:5, 10; stanzas 5 and 10 of a ten-stanza hymn. Italics added for emphasis.

5

The Sacraments and Participation in the Divine Nature

It is impossible to understand Charles Wesley's theology of participation apart from the sacraments of baptism and the Eucharist. Both are a means of grace by which the incarnation is imparted to the life of the Christian and by which and through which God makes divine. The focus is on God and God's action.

Baptism

In stanza 1 of a poem titled "At the Baptism of a Child,"[1] published in *Family Hymns* 1763, Wesley prays that the child through baptism becomes a partaker of God's nature and that the divine image shall be restored.

> 1. God of eternal truth and love,
>   Vouchsafe the promised grace we claim,
> Thine own great ordinance approve,
>   *The child baptized into thy name*
> *Partaker of thy nature make,*
> And give her all thine image back.

Wesley affirms that baptism is an act of God's grace and is integral to the process of participation in God's nature. It embodies God's promised grace claimed by the church, and through it one becomes a partaker of the divine nature. It is a redemptive act in which the lost divine image is restored. Here Wesley's comment is in contrast to St. Gregory Palamas, who speaks of the

---

1. *Family Hymns* 1767, 63-64, Hymn 62:1-5; *PW*, 7: 71-72.

restoration at baptism of the "divine likeness" lost through sin.[2] As noted later in this volume Wesley does not make as sharp a distinction between divine image and divine likeness as one finds in Palamas and other church fathers.

> 2. Born in the dregs of sin and time,
> > These darkest, last, apostate days,
> > Burdened with Adam's curse and crime
> > Thou in thy mercy's arms embrace,
> > And wash out all her guilty load,
> > And quench the brand in Jesus' blood.

Stanza 2 recalls the loss of the divine image through Adam's sin. This emphasis in relationship to baptism is found in St. Athanasius as well: "As we are all from earth and die in Adam, so being regenerated from above of water and Spirit, in the Christ we are all quickened,"[3] though Athanasius does not use the words *curse* and *crime* in reference to Adam's sin. He speaks of human death in Adam, which is, of course, because of sin. George A. Maloney maintains, however, "If we study the ancient ritual of baptism, which today in the Eastern Churches is still received by infants along with Confirmation and the Eucharist, we find no stress placed on the removal of Adam's original sin."[4]

Wesley emphasizes that God's mercy embraces sinners through Christ's sacrifice; they are cleansed and Adam's curse is removed. Baptism is an act of divine initiative (stanzas 3 and 4), a communal ecclesial act (stanza 1), and a realization of salvation from sin (stanza 2).

> 3. Father, if such thy sovereign will,
> > If Jesus *did* the rite enjoin,
> > Annex thy hallowing Spirit's seal,
> > And let the grace attend the sign;
> > The seed of endless life impart,
> > Seize for thy own our infant's heart.

What a prayer for the church to pray for a child at baptism—"The seed of endless life impart, / Seize for thy own our infant's heart"!

2. *On Participation to God*, Coisl. 99, fol. 22; cited in Meyendorff, *Study of Gregory Palamas*, 161.

3. *Four Discourses Against the Arians* 3:26[33].

4. Maloney, *Gold, Frankincense, and Myrrh*, 89.

The Sacraments and Participation

Wesley punctuates the vital role of the Holy Spirit in baptism. It applies the sacred baptismal seal[5] accompanied by God's grace and the imparting of life eternal. Article 27 "Of Baptism" of the 1662 BCP with which Charles Wesley was indeed familiar speaks of the seal of the Holy Ghost at baptism.

> BAPTISM is not only a sign of profession, and mark of difference, whereby Christian men are discerned from others that be not christened, but it is also a sign of Regeneration or New-Birth, whereby, as by an instrument, *they that receive Baptism rightly are grafted into the Church; the promises of the forgiveness of sin, and of our adoption to be the sons of God by the Holy Ghost, are visibly signed and sealed;* Faith is confirmed, and Grace increased by virtue of prayer unto God. The Baptism of young Children is in any wise to be retained in the Church, as most agreeable with the institution of Christ.[6]

This is a perspective assuredly in concert with St. Gregory of Nyssa: "That which creates life in those who are baptized is the Spirit, concerning which the Lord said with his own voice: the Spirit is the giver of life."[7]

How amazing is stanza 4! Wesley would have the church ask, what is God's intent in and through the sacrament of baptism? The last line of the stanza is his answer: "Pardon, and holiness, and heaven." One is pardoned from sin, destined for a life of holiness, and ultimately eternal life.

> 4. Answer on her thy wisdom's end
>   In present and eternal good;
> Whate'er thou didst for us intend,
>   Whate'er thou hast on us bestowed,
> Now to this favour'd babe be given,
> Pardon, and holiness, and heaven.

Since the apostolic age baptism has been by water and the Spirit (Acts 19:5–6) and sealed by the Holy Trinity who fills the baptized with the life divine.

---

5. St. Basil speaks of baptism as "an unbreakable seal" in *Sermons on Moral and Practical Subjects*, 13:5.

6. Italics added for emphasis.

7. St. Gregory of Nyssa, *Concerning the Holy Spirit*, PG 45, 1325A.

> 5. In presence of thy heavenly host
>   Thyself we faithfully require;
> Come, Father, Son, and Holy Ghost,
>   By blood, by water, and by fire,
> And fill up all thy human shrine,
> And seal our souls for ever thine.

Does Wesley really mean that all for which he and the church pray at the baptism of a child actually transpires? Might one say that he is simply praying for these things on behalf of the child with the hope of their future fulfillment and, hence, the child's participation in the divine nature at baptism is not a present reality? Is the poem simply an expression of hope for the child's future and the pilgrimage toward deification and holiness she will experience?

Perhaps a poem left unpublished at Wesley's death aids in answering the above questions. It is based on Acts 19:5, "They were baptized in the name of the Lord Jesus." The one-stanza poem reads as Charles Wesley's own testimony to the power and effect of participation in the divine nature at baptism.

> Truly baptized into the name
>   Of Jesus I have been,
> *Who partner of his nature am*
>   And saved indeed from sin.
> *Thy nature, Lord, through faith I feel,*
>   Thy love revealed in me.
> In me thy full salvation dwell,
>   To all eternity.[8]

In baptism, avers Wesley, one experiences the full salvation of God and becomes a partner of God's nature. After an opening statement regarding the experience of the rite of baptism, the next four lines focus on the partnership with God's nature. Having been baptized into the name of Jesus, he says, "Who partner of his nature *am*." This is a present reality. One is a partner of God's nature and has been redeemed from sin. This is a central facet of Wesleyan theology and many of the church fathers.

Then Wesley moves to the experience of God's nature when he says, "Thy nature, Lord, through faith I *feel*, / Thy love revealed in me." To feel

---

8. The poem is from MSACTS and was published for the first time in *UP* 2:379–80. Italics added for emphasis.

The Sacraments and Participation

God's nature is to be filled with love—God's love. Such love within the redeemed is the evidence of the indwelling nature of God.

Therefore, for Charles Wesley deification is an essential aspect of baptism, as an additional hymn titled "Come Father, Son, and Holy Ghost"[9] to which Wesley gave the subtitle "To be sung at Baptism" underscores.

> 1. Come Father, Son, and Holy Ghost,
>   Revealed in the baptismal flood,
> Joint Saviour thou of sinners lost,
>   Descend, the one eternal God.
>
> 2. Now in thy own appointed hour,
>   Thy own appointed means, appear,
> That all may tremble at thy power,
>   And own the triune God is here.
>
> 3. For these thy ransomed ones we claim
>   The grace which glorious life imparts,
> Their souls baptize into thy name,
>   *And stamp thine image on their hearts.*
>
> 4. Into thy fold this moment take,
>   True witness of their sins forgiven,
> *And partners of thy nature make,*
>   And partners of thy throne in heaven.

In this hymn Wesley emphasizes the unified action of the Holy Trinity (Father, Son, and Holy Spirit) in baptism. The Trinity, the one eternal God, is the "joint Saviour" of lost sinners. This is an enduring emphasis of the church fathers. St. Cyril of Alexandria, for example, stresses that we participate in the life of the Holy Trinity through baptism. "They who by faith in Christ attain unto sonship with God, are baptized into nought originate, but into the Holy Trinity Itself, through the Word as Mediator."[10]

---

9. From Osborn, *PW*, 8:441. Osborn indicates that the manuscript source was then in the possession of C. H. Waring, esq. Its present location is unknown. See website: http://www.divinity.duke.edu/initiatives-centers/cswt/wesley-texts/manuscript-verse. See Assorted Looseleaf Manuscript Verse, p. 4. Italics added for emphasis.

10. St. Cyril of Alexandria, *Commentary on the Gospel According to John*, 1:12–14a; cited in Keating, *Deification and Grace*, 43–44. See also https://ia600400.us.archive.org/1/items/CyrilOfAlexandriaCommentaryOnJohnVolume1Tr.P.E.Pusey1874/cyril.pdf.

Stanza 2 stresses the divine initiative in baptism—it transpires at God's "own appointed hour" and "own appointed means." However, the church also has a distinctive role. Its members "claim / The grace which glorious life imparts." God extends the grace through Christ, and the church claims the grace for all baptized in God's name, but it is God who stamps the divine image in the hearts of the baptized.

There can be no question about the present efficacy of the divine action, at least according to Wesley's prayer in stanza 4. He prays, "Into Thy fold *this moment* take." There is an immediate effect of baptism. The baptized are taken into God's fold and sins are forgiven. They become members of Christ's body. And Wesley goes further: "*And partners of Thy nature make, / And partners of Thy throne in heaven.*" The baptized share in the divine nature and inherit life eternal. Thus baptism is "an ontological event; it refashions and completes [man's] created being."[11]

Wesley's words, particularly in stanza 4, resonate with the words of St. Dionysius the Areopagite: "Through this divine-like joining together of all, baptism also grants to us communion and unification with God."[12]

Holy Communion

One of the most important studies of John and Charles Wesley's joint publication, *HLS* 1745, that explores the patristic roots of the volume is by Geoffrey Wainwright, "'Our Elder Brethren Join': The Patristic Revival in England," which appeared in the 1994 issue of *The Proceedings of The Charles Wesley Society*. He examines to what extent the hymns reflect ritual features "present or implied in the eucharistic liturgy of *Apostolic Constitutions* VIII, of the 1549 BCP, and of Thomas Deacon's *Compleat Collection of Devotions*. Three of them in particular are significant for the *HLS* 1745 and the patristic roots of that collection: the water, the oblation, and the epiclesis."[13] He then shows how the themes of many of the hymns fit into the structure of the so-called Clementine liturgy, a few other ancient liturgies, and are in concert with a number of church fathers.[14] Wainwright

---

11. Nellas, *Deification in Christ*, 121.
12. *Concerning What is Performed in the Synaxis*, PG 3, 424CD.
13. Wainwright, "Our Elder Brethren Join," 8.
14. In an article titled "The Wesleys' *Hymns on the Lord's Supper* and Orthodoxy," published in the 1995 edition of the *Proceedings of The Charles Wesley Society*, Leonid Kishkovsky delineates four themes—the Holy Trinity, the Holy Spirit, eucharistic piety, and the use of Old Testament images—that find mutual resonance in the Wesley

The Sacraments and Participation

further states, "Whether directly or by way of Thomas Deacon's *Compleat Collection of Devotions*, the Wesleys' *Hymns on the Lord's Supper* reflect a knowledge of the eucharistic liturgy of the *Apostolic Constitution* VIII."[15]

Wainwright notes one example of a patristic link in the eucharistic hymns having to do with participation in the divine nature. "In hymn 32 ('Jesu, to Thee for help we call'), the Wesleys reflect the notion of St. Irenaeus and St. Athanasius that the Son of God became the Son of Man so that the sons of men might become sons of God:

> Thou God of sanctifying love,
> Adam descended from above,
> ...
> We here thy nature shall retrieve,
> And all Thy heavenly image bear."[16]

Charles Wesley unequivocally shares the Orthodox view that through the sacrament of Holy Communion one is deified and God's nature is made known. Here he stands close to St. Ephrem the Syrian, for whom Holy Communion was the cradle of deification.

In *HLS* 1745 Charles Wesley writes,

> 2. Obedient to thy gracious word
>   We break the hallowed bread,
> Commemorate thee, our dying Lord,
>   And trust on thee to feed.
>
> 3. Now, Saviour, now thyself reveal,
>   *And make thy nature known,*
> *Affix the sacramental seal,*
>   *And stamp us for thine own.*
>
> 4. The tokens of thy dying love,
>   O let us all receive,
> And feel the quick'ning Spirit move,
>   And sensibly relieve.

---

eucharistic hymns and the liturgies of St. John Chrysostom and St. Basil the Great. He also notes significant differences, such as the predominance of Old Testament references and absence of the theme of the resurrection of Christ in these hymns.

15. Wainwright, "Our Elder Brethren Join," 17.
16. Ibid., 28.

> 8. Now, Lord, on us thy flesh bestow,
>   And let us drink thy blood,
> Till all our souls are filled below
>   With all the life of God.[17]

In another hymn from the same collection he states,

> 2. What streams of sweetness from the bowl
>   Surprize and deluge all my soul,
>   Sweetness which is, and *makes divine,*
>   Surely from God's right-hand they flow,
>   From thence derived to earth below,
>   To cheer us with immortal wine.[18]

God, who links human and divine nature and enables us to participate in the divine nature, *makes divine* through the elements of bread and wine at the Eucharist. Wesley accentuates this reality further with these lines:

> Christ in us; in him we see
> Fullness of the Deity,
> Beam of the Eternal Beam;
> *Life divine we taste in him.*[19]

Cyril of Alexandria says, "And since the flesh of the savior has become life-giving (as being united to that which is by nature life, the Word of God), then we have life in ourselves, we too united to it as it to the indwelling Word."[20]

Let there be no mistake—Wesley says quite clearly that as we partake of the immortal elements of bread and wine, God makes the divine nature known.

> Jesus, Master of the feast,
>   The feast itself thou art,
> Now receive thy meanest guest,
>   And comfort every heart:

---

17. *HLS* 1745, 23–24, Hymn 30:2–4, 8; four stanzas of an eight-stanza hymn. Italics added for emphasis.

18. Ibid., 133, Hymn 160:2; stanza 2 of a six-stanza hymn. Italics added for emphasis.

19. Ibid., 138, Hymn 164:7; stanza 7 of an eight-stanza hymn. Italics added for emphasis.

20. *Comm. In Io.* 6:53 (Pusey 1:418); cited in Keating, *Deification and Grace*, 55.

> Give us living bread to eat,
>   Manna that from heaven comes down,
> Fill us with immortal meat,
>   *And make thy nature known.*[21]

Alexander Golitzin's description of the sacramental views of St. Symeon the New Theologian in *Discourse* III are equally appropriate to Charles Wesley in the light of the above poems: "He feels no conflict between his devotion to and encounter with Christ 'in the heart' and the Lord's presence in the consecrated elements on the altar. Communion with Christ in the heart and at the altar are reciprocal. Better, they are one and the same mystery."[22]

The theological thrust of the above eucharistic hymns of Wesley is indeed congruent with St. Gregory of Nyssa's view of deification through the Eucharist.

> Since, then, that God-sustaining flesh partook for its substance and support of this particular nourishment also, and since the God who was manifested infused himself into perishable humanity for this purpose, viz. that by this communion with Deity mankind might at the same time be deified, for this end it is that, by dispensation of his grace, he disseminates himself in every believer through that flesh, whose substance comes from bread and wine, blending himself with the bodies of believers, to secure that, by this union with the immortal, man, too, may be a sharer in incorruption.[23]

It is not surprising that Wesley rejoices in the memory of the "saints of former days" who "every joyful day received" the Eucharist, for they were daily sharing in the divine nature through the sacrament. With every Eucharist they taste life divine in Christ.

In Charles's treatise "And upon the first Day of the Week," which is based on Acts 20:7, he states, "I would observe that the breaking of bread or celebrating the Eucharist is by the text expressly declared to be the end and design of the Christians meeting together."[24] He extends this thought further in a lengthy poem by stressing daily communion.

---

21. *HLS* 1745, 72, Hymn 84:3; stanza 3 of a four-stanza hymn. Italics added for emphasis.

22. Golitzin, *On the Mystical Life*, 3:111.

23. *Cat. Or.* 37 (*NPNF*^{2} 5:506).

24. Wesley, *Sermons*, 282.

1. Happy the saints of former days,
    Who first continued in the word,
  A simple, lowly, loving race,
    True followers of their Lamb-like Lord.

2. In holy fellowship they lived,
    Nor would from the commandment move,
  But every joyful day received
    The tokens of expiring love.

The line "But every joyful day received / The tokens of expiring love" reminds one of St. Symeon the New Theologian, who received Holy Communion each day during his monastic life and said, "Blessed are those who are nourished with Christ every day."[25]

3. Not then above their Master wise,
    They simply in his paths remained,
  And called to mind his sacrifice,
    With steadfast faith and love unfeigned.

4. From house to house they broke the bread
    Impregnated with Life divine,
  And drank the Spirit of their Head
    Transmitted in the sacred wine.[26]

The broken bread, the body of Christ, says Wesley, is "impregnated with the Life divine," hence those who partake of it are recipients of the divine life. Furthermore, the Spirit is "transmitted in the sacred wine." Thus, to refuse participation in the Eucharist is to refuse participation in the divine life and the Spirit. Here Wesley stresses an ecclesiological dimension of deification—it is a communal experience for the gathered church. As it receives the elements, it participates corporately in the divine life.

---

25. Symeon the New Theologian, *Ethical Discourses*, 10.790-91.

26. *HLS* 1745, 139, Hymn 166:1-4; stanzas 1-4 of a twenty-two stanza poem. Italics added for emphasis.

The Epiclesis

Not only is the Spirit "transmitted in the sacred wine," Wesley in a brief two-stanza hymn invokes the Holy Spirit to infuse life and power into the bread and wine.

> 1. Come, Holy Ghost, thine influence shed,
>   And realize the sign,
> Thy life infuse into the bread,
>   Thy power into the wine.
>
> 2. Effectual let the tokens prove,
>   And made by heavenly art
> Fit channels to convey thy love
>   To every faithful heart.[27]

In the hymn cited above, "Come, Holy Ghost, thine influence shed," Wesley created a lyrical epiclesis. He does not use the liturgical words "bless and sanctify"; rather, he implores the Holy Spirit to infuse life into the bread and power into the wine. This is the realization of the Spirit's activity in the Eucharist and is most certainly in concert with the liturgical epiclesis included in the liturgies of Eastern Churches.

The hymn implies that the life infused is the life of Christ. Thus, the Holy Spirit enlivens the elements. Wesley's words remind one of the invocation of the Holy Spirit in the 1549 BCP of Thomas Cranmer: "Hear us (O merciful Father) we beseech thee; and with thy Holy Spirit and word vouchsafe to bless and sanctify these thy gifts and creatures of Bread and Wine, that they may be unto us the Body and Blood of thy most dearly beloved Son Jesus Christ."[28] Given the ongoing discord in the seventeenth and eighteenth centuries over the significance of the epiclesis, the prayer did not survive in the 1662 revision of the BCP, the one used by the Wesleys. They were no doubt aware of the controversy over this prayer, especially as regards differences between the Greek and Latin Churches[29] pertaining to the form and moment of consecration of the sacrament. Their awareness

---

27. Ibid., 51, Hymn 72.
28. BCP, 1549. The quotation may be found on p. 218 at the top of the left-hand column.
29. See Taft, "The Epiclesis Question in the Light of the Orthodox and Catholic *Lex Orandi* Traditions."

was perhaps due in part to the fact that they were greatly influenced by the Nonjurors,[30] who wanted to revive many of the practices of the early church, including the use of an epiclesis, which was retained in many of the Eastern rites—for example, Liturgy of St. James, Liturgy of St. John Chrysostom, Liturgy of St. Basil the Great—though not in an identical formulation. More Protestant-leaning Anglicans were opposed to the prayer and had lesser sympathies for its use in the Roman and Eastern Churches.

Geoffrey Wainwright avers: "Even more remarkable is the invocation of the Holy Spirit as 'witness of the sufferings' of Christ, an image drawn directly from *AC* [*Apostolic Constitutions*] VIII.12.39 (*ton matura tôn pathêmatôn tou Kuriou Iêsou*). It is in this capacity that the Holy Spirit becomes the Divine Agent of the eucharistic anamnesis, the 'Recorder' or 'Remembrancer' at the royal court."[31] These comments are followed by the quotation of the following lines from Hymn 16:

1. Come, thou everlasting Spirit,
    Bring to every thankful mind
   All the Saviour's dying merit
    All his suffering for mankind:
   True recorder of his passion,
    Now the living faith impart,
   Now reveal his great salvation,
    Preach his gospel to our heart.

2. Come, thou witness of his dying,
    Come, remembrancer divine,
   Let us feel thy power applying
    Christ to every soul and mine.[32]

Through the influence of John Clayton, a member of the Wesleys' Oxford group, John Wesley came into contact with some of the Manchester Nonjurors. One of them, whom he met in 1733, was Bishop Thomas Deacon (1697–1753), who published the volume *Compleat Collection of Devotions: Taken from the Apostolic Constitutions, the Ancient Liturgies, and the Common Prayer Book of the Church of England* (1734), which John Wesley

---

30. See Cornwall, "The Later Nonjurors and the Theological Basis of the Usages Controversy."

31. Wainright, "Our Elder Brethren Join," 27.

32. *HLS* 1745, 13, Hymn 16.

read on his voyage to Georgia in 1735. Interestingly, he had contributed to the volume excerpts from his "Essay upon the Stationary Fasts." Deacon was a physician and liturgical scholar who reintroduced ancient aspects of the Eucharist, including the epiclesis and the oblation. Though John Wesley must have known these aspects of Deacon's liturgical work, especially his new liturgy, "The Order of the Divine Offices of the Orthodox British Church," this was not sufficient to persuade him to include them in the edition of the *Sunday Service* he prepared for Methodists in the American colonies.[33]

Participation Realized through Holy Communion

Charles Wesley claims that the Lord's Supper was instituted so that we might participate in the divine nature. It is by no means merely a sign, merely a remembrance. It is a participation in the divine, an experience of union with God: "One with thyself my soul to make" through the presence of Christ in the sacred meal. In emphasizing that one's body, soul, and spirit are joined "inseparably one with thine" (i.e., with God's), Wesley was stating much more than a comfortable, spiritualized concept. He articulated a divine/human oneness that is inseparable! Indeed, "Christ instituted this sacrament so that his disciples could partake of his divine nature."[34]

> Saviour, thou didst the Mystery give
> *That I thy nature might partake,*
> Thou bidst me outward signs receive,
> One with thyself my soul to make,
> My body, soul and spir't to join
> Inseparably one with thine.[35]

As partakers of the sacrifice of Christ in Holy Communion we share in the divine nature and are empowered by the elements of bread and wine, infused with life and power, to live a life of holiness.

---

33. *John Wesley's Sunday Service of Methodists in North America.*
34. Loyer, "Memorial, Means, and Pledge," 98
35. *HLS* 1745, 39, Hymn 54:3; stanza 3 of a five-stanza hymn. Italics added for emphasis.

> O that we now thy flesh may eat,
>   Its virtue really receive,
> Impowered by this immortal meat
>   The life of holiness to live:
> *Partakers of thy sacrifice*
>   *O may we all thy nature share,*
> Till to the holiest place we rise,
>   And keep the feast for ever there.[36]

It is indeed interesting that many discussions of Charles Wesley's interpretation of the Eucharist ignore the concept of participation in the divine nature. There seems to be a preoccupation with presenting his theology of the Eucharist as "Protestant" in its perspectives.

In discussing "The Doctrine of the Lord's Supper" in his volume *The Sacrament of the Lord's Supper in Early Methodism*, John C. Bowmer makes no mention whatsoever of sharing in the divine nature through participation in the sacred meal. He comments, "Wesley had little liking for mysticism, but he could not evade the mystical element in the Lord's Supper."[37] Then he cites stanza 3 of Hymn 54 from *HLS* 1745 just quoted above, which begins, "Saviour, thou didst this Mystery give, / That I thy nature might partake." However, he completely ignores commenting on the meaning of these lines. Instead, he moves immediately to a Pauline comment on the blood of Christ, which is inappropriate to the text just cited. Although Bowmer mentions the possible influence of the church fathers on Charles Wesley via the Nonjurors as regards the epiclesis prayer[38] created by Charles in the hymn "Come, Holy Ghost, thine influence shed," he makes no mention of deification or what it means to partake of the divine nature. Even as he quotes Charles's lines "One, with the undivided Bread" and "One with the Living Bread Divine," Bowmer is unable to move beyond emphasizing the role of sacrifice in early Methodist eucharistic theology. Then he gives away his own bias: "In his thought of the Death of Christ as a Sacrifice and of the Eucharist as it implies a Sacrifice, Wesley's Protestantism is never in

---

36. Ibid., 95, Hymn 112:3; stanza 3 of a three-stanza hymn. Italics added for emphasis.

37. Bowmer, *Sacrament of the Lord's Supper*, 175. Charles Wesley does speak of the "snare of mysticism" in *MSJ*, 2:646.

38. Bowmer, *Sacrament of the Lord's Supper*, 86–87.

doubt."³⁹ Unfortunately, his misguided presupposition has not allowed him to read the fullness of Charles Wesley's poetry.

In J. Ernest Rattenbury's seminal study, *The Eucharistic Hymns of John and Charles Wesley*, there is a brief section in chapter 7 that addresses the subject of "union with Christ." Rattenbury states, "The union of Christ with us indicates the oneness of the whole Church of Christ. We are not a mere collection of individuals, but a collective body; one temple, one body, one vine."⁴⁰ He interprets the following lines of Wesley as "a very characteristic description of the collectivity of the Church":⁴¹

> 1. How happy are thy servants, Lord,
>   Who thus remember thee!
>   What tongue can tell our sweet accord,
>   Our perfect harmony!
>
> 2. Who thy Mysterious Supper share,
>   Here at thy table fed,
>   Many, and yet but One we are,
>   One undivided Bread.
>
> 3. *One with the Living Bread Divine,*
>   Which now by faith we eat,
>   Our hearts, and minds, and spirits join,
>   And all in Jesus meet.⁴²

Rattenbury, however, has interpreted Wesley's text primarily in the context of the oneness of the church as the body of Christ, and he makes no mention of deification. When Wesley avers in line 1 of stanza 3 that we are "one with the Living Bread Divine," he is unquestionably intimating more than an earthly unity of the church universal. Wesley's perspective is very close to the view of the Eucharist expressed by Kallistos Ware: "It is above all through Communion that the Christian is made one with and in Christ, 'christified,' 'ingodded' or 'deified.'"⁴³

---

39. Ibid., 181.
40. Rattenbury, *Eucharistic Hymns*, 130.
41. Ibid.
42. *HLS* 1745, 138, Hymn 165:1–3; stanzas 1–3 of a four-stanza hymn. Italics added for emphasis.
43. Ware, *Orthodox Way*, 109.

As in the case of Wesley's view of partaking of the divine nature through the incarnation, his view of being a partaker of the life divine through participation in Holy Communion also can only be understood in the context of the Mystery, which cannot be fully comprehended. How is one's nature transformed into the divine? This remains a mystery, but the faithful are sustained in the Eucharist by God, who mystically links human and divine natures through the elements of bread and wine, and thus as Charles Wesley says, "makes divine." Hence, there is in Wesley what Russell finds in Athanasius, namely, "the sacramental character of deification."[44] Wesley's views are also congruent with those of St. Cyril of Alexandria whereby baptism and Holy Communion are the means through which believers receive the divine life.[45]

---

44. Russell, *Doctrine of Deification*, 185.
45. See Keating, *The Appropriation of Divine Life in Cyril of Alexandria*.

6

The Trinity and Participation in the Divine Nature

Charles Wesley was an ardent defender of Trinitarian theology. While the hymn texts cited in this chapter are not exclusively from the volume *Trinity Hymns* 1767, it is important to note their relationship to William Jones's (1726–1800) tract *The Catholic Doctrine of a Trinity, proved by above an Hundred Short and Clear Arguments*[1] (1756), on which the majority of Wesley's hymns are based. Jones's work was written in opposition to the rise of Arianism in early eighteenth-century England, as well as the infiltration of Socinian, Unitarian, and Deist ideas. Jones explicitly opposed Samuel Clarke (1675–1729), who averred in *The Scripture Doctrine of the Trinity* (1712) that the Trinity is one, not three persons: Father, Son, and Holy Spirit.

In 136 of the 188 hymns in *Trinity Hymns* 1767 Wesley follows closely the outline of Jones's work and a broad range of his theological emphases. One finds in these hymns a strong defense of the tenets of the Nicene faith of the Church of England. Wesley unequivocally opposed Arianism, as well as Latitudinarians for whom defense of the church's doctrine was not a priority. Just as the controversy with Arianism provided the content for the development of Athanasian theology,[2] so it is with Wesley's theology of the Trinity expressed in *Trinity Hymns* 1767.[3]

Though there were hosts of advocates and opponents of the doctrine of the Trinity in early eighteenth-century Anglicanism, Wesley found

---

1. For the importance of Jones's volume, its influence on Charles Wesley, and his response to it, see Allchin, "The Trinity in the Teaching of Charles Wesley."
2. See Kharlamov, "Rhetorical Application of *Theosis*," 118.
3. See Quantrille, "The Triune God in the Hymns of Charles Wesley."

Jones's arguments so convincing that he developed an entire volume of poetry based on the latter's apologetic for the doctrine of the Trinity.

In *Trinity Hymns* 1767 one finds a strong link between deification and the Trinity. However, this emphasis of Wesley has been scarcely mentioned in the study of these hymns.

Trinitarian Divine Nature

In a short poem based on Num 6:24, "The LORD bless thee and keep thee," Wesley emphasizes that the divine nature of which we partake is Trinitarian. This he makes vividly clear when he prays for the restoration of God's nature.

> Come, Father, Son, and Holy-Ghost,
>   One God in Persons Three,
> Bring back the heavenly blessing, lost
>   By all mankind, and me:
> *Thy favour, and thy nature too,*
>   *To me, to all restore,*
> Forgive, and after God renew,
>   And keep us evermore.[4]

Restorer of the Divine Image and Giver of Love

In the following poem he addresses the Holy Trinity as the "Restorer" of the divine image humankind has lost. In stanza 6 Wesley affirms that it is God's Spirit, the "sure indwelling guide," that sanctifies and stamps the lost divine image in our hearts.

> 1. Come Father, Son, and Holy Ghost,
>   Restorer of thine image lost,
>   The flaming sword remove;
>   Teach me thine image to regain,
>   And to my docile heart explain
>   The mystery of love.

---

4. *Scripture Hymns* 1762, 1:62, Hymn 299. Italics added for emphasis.

The Trinity and Participation

2. I now perceive thy love's design;
   Thou didst again in council join,
     Thy name to re-impress,
   Anew thy creature to create,
   And raise me to my first estate
     In perfect righteousness.

3. To execute thy kind intent,
   Jehovah from Jehovah sent
     Left his eternal throne,
   A Man of Griefs, he stained the tree,
   Saviour of all, he laid for me
     The precious ransom down.

4. The Spirit purchased with his blood,
   By Father and by Son bestowed
     Doth now in man reside;
   For us he strongly intercedes,
   Us into all thy counsel leads
     Our sure indwelling guide.

5. Pardon he[5] on our conscience seals,
   Thy good and welcome will reveals
     To save a world by grace:
   He marks us for salvation's heirs,
   And moulds and fashions, and prepares
     To see thine open face.

6. *He sanctifies,* without respect
   Of high or low, his own elect
     Regenerate from above,
   Into thy glorious form converts,
   And stamps thine image on our hearts
     In purity and love.

---

5. The pronoun "he" in stanzas 5–7 refers to the "Spirit" in stanza 4.

> 7. *O wouldst thou stamp it now on mine*
> *The name and character divine*
> *The holy One in Three!*
> *Come, Father, Son, and Spirit, give*
> *Thy love,—thyself: and lo! I live*
> *Imparadised in thee.*[6]

Stanza 7 is a Trinitarian prayer *par excellence* that invites the Trinity to give itself—that is, love—to those in prayer, that they might live "imparadised in" the Holy Trinity. It anticipates the possibility of sanctification perhaps on this side of the grave with the words "O wouldst thou stamp it *now* on mine."

John Meyendorff eloquently articulates the life of love in the fellowship of the Trinity in these words: "Deification or theosis of the Greek fathers is an acceptance of human persons within a divine life, which already is itself a fellowship of love between three co-eternal Persons, welcoming humanity within their mutuality."[7] This is life imparadised in the Holy Trinity.

Anticipation of Perfect Righteousness

In another prayer, Hymn 48 of the concluding section of *Trinity Hymns* 1767, which is a plea for the communication of God's nature, Wesley emphasizes the importance of love and purity for the anticipation of perfect righteousness, qualification for salvation, and the vision of the Trinity.

> 1. Tri-une God, the New-Creator
> Of our fallen souls appear,
> O communicate thy nature,
> Raise us to thy image *here*,
> In true holiness renewed,
> Spotless portraitures of God.

---

6. *Trinity Hymns* 1767, 113–14, Hymn 30. Italics added for emphasis.
7. Meyendorff, "Theosis in the Eastern Christian Tradition," 475.

2. By a blest anticipation
>Of thy perfect righteousness,

Qualify us for salvation
>Vessels of celestial grace,

Meet by love and purity

God without a veil to see.[8]

Geoffrey Wainwright rightly sees this "as a prolepsis of the vision of God that will be granted in heaven."[9]

Knowledge of the Trinity

As partakers of God's nature, it is the Holy Trinity we come to know.

>Father of me, and all mankind,
>>And all the hosts above,
>
>Let every understanding mind
>>Unite to praise thy love,
>
>*To know thy nature and thy name,*
>>One God in Persons Three,
>
>And glorify the great I AM
>>Thro' all eternity.[10]

In this poem Wesley pleads, "Let every understanding mind / Unite to praise thy love." We shall return later to his equation of God's nature and name with the word *love*. Here Wesley emphasizes the value of human intellect in the process of participation in the divine nature; it embodies a cognitive dimension. While human intellect cannot of itself enable the participation, the "understanding mind" is a vital element in responding to God's nature, that is, love. Those with understanding minds join to praise God's love and "to know" God's nature and name. Who is the God one unites to know? The Holy Trinity, "One God in Persons Three."

---

8. *Trinity Hymns* 1767, 127–28, Hymn 48:1–2; stanzas 1 and 2 of a three-stanza hymn. Italics added for emphasis.

9. Wainwright, "Trinitarian Theology and Wesleyan Holiness," 69. See also his *Eucharist and Eschatology.*

10. *Scripture Hymns* 1762, 2:220, Hymn 342, based on Luke 11:2, "Our Father which art in heaven, hallowed be thy name." Italics added for emphasis.

Corporate Experience of the Trinity

In Charles Wesley's view one may not participate in the divine nature through one person of the Trinity alone: Father, Son, or Holy Spirit. It is a corporate experience of the Godhead.

> The promise stands for ever sure,
>   And we shall in thine image shine,
> *Partakers of a nature pure,*
>   *Holy, and perfect, and divine,*
> In Spirit joined to thee the Son,
> As thou art with thy Father one.[11]

When one partakes of the pure, divine nature, one is united with the Holy Trinity and is joined to the Godhead, as the Father, Son, and Spirit are joined as one. This union with God, however, is a mystical experience that cannot be fully grasped. The union of mortal and immortal results in a cosmic communion with the Holy Trinity.[12]

Transcript of the Trinity

> 1. Father, Son, and Spirit, hear
>   Faith's effectual, fervent prayer,
>   Hear, and our petitions seal;
>   Let us now the answer feel.
>
>   *Mystically one with thee,*
>   *Transcript of the Trinity,*
>   Thee let all our nature own
>   One in Three, and Three in One.[13]

What does Wesley mean that we are to be transcripts of the Trinity? The divine nature presented in human form. As with participation in God's nature through the Eucharist, this too is a mystical experience ("Mystically

---

11. *HSP* 1742, 234; stanza 12 of a thirteen-stanza poem. The poem is based on Isa 40:8, "The word of our God shall stand forever." Italics added for emphasis.

12. See compatible comments of John Wesley in "The New Creation," Sermon 64.

13. *HSP* 1740, 188, Part 1:1; stanza 1 of a seven-stanza poem. Each stanza has eight lines. Italics added for emphasis. John Wesley omitted the four lines beginning "Mystically one with thee," as well as stanza 5, from the 1780 *Collection*, Hymn 501, 690.

one with thee"), namely, to be shaped in the divine nature while yet being fully human. This involves the divine ownership of "all our nature." There is an intimate bond of the divine and human natures as intimate as the bond of the Holy Trinity—"One in Three, and Three in One."

Wesley continues in stanzas 4 and 5 of the same poem that is titled "The Communion of Saints."

> 4. One with God, the source of bliss,
> Ground of our communion this,
> Life of all that live below,
> Let thy emanations flow,
>
> Rise eternal in our heart:
> Thou our only Eden art;
> Father, Son, and Holy Ghost,
> Be to us what Adam lost.
>
> 5. Bold we ask thro' Christ the Son,
> Thou, O Christ, art all our own;
> Our exalted flesh we see
> To the Godhead joined in thee:
>
> Glorious now thy heaven we share,
> Thou art here, and we are there,
> We participate of thine,
> *Human nature of divine.*[14]

Participating in God's nature does not deny human nature but affirms it. As St. Gregory Palamas asserted, "The Logos became flesh, and the flesh became Logos, even though neither abandoned its own proper nature."[15]

Inner Activity of the Trinity

There is a fascinating poem in Charles Wesley's *Preparation for Death* 1772, in which he dwells on the importance of the inner life. It emphasizes the

---

14. Ibid., 189, Part 1:4, 5; stanzas 4 and 5 of a seven-stanza poem. Italics added for emphasis.
15. See Mantzaridis, *Deification of Man*, 29.

necessity of God's laws being written within, and if one does not share in the divine nature in this life, one cannot inherit eternal life.

> 3. I want thy laws engraved within,
>   Thy chaste antipathy to sin,
>   Thy love of purity:
>   *Unless I here thy nature share,*
>   I know, my soul can never bear
>   A holy God to see.
>
> 4. How shall I, Lord, the meetness gain?
>   Thy only blood from every stain
>   *Can make my nature pure:*
>   And shed for all the sinful race,
>   It bought the pardon and the grace
>   That makes salvation sure.[16]

Further, he stresses the inner activity of the Holy Trinity: pardon through the death of Christ, perfect holiness through the indwelling Spirit, and being "fashioned after my Creator." This experience culminates in the eloquent summary of participation in the divine nature: "God as I am known to know."

> 2. Thro' thy death and righteous merit
>   Pardon still I hope t'obtain,
>   Thro' thy pure indwelling Spirit
>   Perfect holiness to gain:
>   *Partner of thy sinless nature,*
>   All thy spotless mind to show,
>   Fashioned after my Creator,
>   God as I am known to know.[17]

In the fourth stanza of this same poem his diction is unsurpassable in the invitation to the indwelling of the Holy Trinity. He pleads, "Draw me now into my centre"! There is no egocentrism in Wesley's view. The center to which he refers is the Father, Son, and Spirit who enter and seal his soul forever as God's.

---

16. *Preparation for Death* 1772, 33, Hymn 31:3, 4; stanzas 3 and 4 of a six-stanza hymn. Italics added for emphasis.

17. Ibid., 32, Hymn 30:2; stanza 2 of a four-stanza hymn. Italics added for emphasis.

The Trinity and Participation

    4. If thou hast in mercy caught me,
        Thee that I may apprehend,
    If to this thyself has wrought me,
        That I may to heaven ascend,
    Draw me now into my centre;
        Into thy ambitious shrine,
    Father, Son, and Spirit enter,
        Seal my soul for ever thine.[18]

The Trinity at the Center

Wesley knew that human beings are not the central focus of their existence. God is. The process of participation places God, the Holy Trinity, at the center. Hence, humility is requisite to its realization. This is why he writes,

    O may I never take the praise
        Or my own glory spread,
    If made thine instrument to raise
        A sinner from the dead!
    O may I never boast my own
        Successful ministry,
    But sink forgotten and unknown,
        And swallowed up in thee![19]

The example of Christ's humility, "who humbled [himself] for our sake," is eloquently expressed by Charles Wesley in his interpretation of the pivotal New Testament passage that occupies an interesting place among many scholars[20] of the Eastern Church regarding deification, 2 Pet 1:4:

---

18. Ibid., 32–33, Hymn 30:4; stanza 4 of a four-stanza hymn. Italics added for emphasis.

19. *Scripture Hymns* 1762, 2:218, Hymn 336, based on Luke 8:56, "He charged them that they should tell no man what was done."

20. See Russell, *Fellow Workers with God*, 65–69, for the interpretations of 2 Pet 1:4 by Origen, St. Athanasius, St. Cyril of Alexandria, and St. Gregory Palamas. Daniel Keating observes, "Though 2 Peter 1:4 is an important biblical affirmation of what deification was understood to mean, the early Church did not build its notion of deification on this text. When the Fathers employ 2 Peter 1:4, they typically apply it to indicate just what the formula of exchange describes: our participation in the divine life through Christ and in the Holy Spirit, by which we become and truly are 'sons of God'" (*Deification and Grace*, 36–37).

Partakers of the Life Divine

"Whereby are given unto us exceeding great and precious promises, that by these you might be partakers of the divine nature, having escaped the corruption that is in the world through lust." This biblical passage along with Heb 3:14, "For we are made partakers of Christ, if we hold the beginning of our confidence steadfast unto the end," precedes the following poem, which appears in the section "Hymns on the Divinity of Christ" in *Hymns on the Trinity* 1767.

> 1. *All who partake of Christ, partake*
>   *The nature properly divine*
> Of him, who humbled for our sake,
>   Us with himself vouchsafed to join;
> And in his single person showed
> The substance both of man and God.
>
> 2. The precious promises in him
>   Are all contained and verified;
> And fashioned like the God supreme,
>   Whoe'er in Christ by faith abide,
> Th'essential holiness they share,
> The image of the heavenly bear.
>
> 3. *Jesus the Lord, thy nature pure*
>   *To us, as capable, impart,*
> And thus our hallowed hearts assure
>   That thou the true Jehovah art,
> And wilt thro' death our leader be,
> Our God thro' all eternity.[21]

In this poem Wesley addresses the centrality of the transformation of human nature in Christ. Those who partake of Christ, partake of the divine nature. For our sakes he humbled himself and joined himself to us. In other words, he took on human flesh like ours. He entered into an intimate relationship with us. Being joined to him, we are joined to God. "Christ raises us to intimacy with the Father because he shares his being with the Father in one sense and with us in another."[22]

---

21. *Trinity Hymns* 1767, 33–34, Hymn 50.
22. Russell, *Fellow Workers with God*, 68.

The Trinity and Participation

What Nancy J. Hudson has said of the Trinitarian theology of St. Maximus the Confessor could most certainly be said of Charles Wesley's theology:

> The significance of his [Maximus'] understanding of the Trinity for theosis is that it places the Christological element at its very heart. The Son was present at creation, at the moment when the world was made for deification. He is not a secondary level of divinity with his own ontological status whose purpose was to retrieve a fallen human spirit. Instead, he is himself both the one who destined human being for theosis and the vehicle for the realization of that destiny. There is no gap between the God of creation and the God of redemption.[23]

Wesley says, "All who partake of Christ, partake / The nature properly divine." And who is "the nature properly divine"? The Holy Trinity. Like St. Maximus the Confessor, Wesley's understanding of the Trinity for participation in the divine nature places Christology at its very heart.

In stanza 2 we learn something about the nature of this relationship. We share the holiness of the divine and bear the heavenly image, that is, the image of God. If we bear the image of God, this is the basis of our conscious relationship with God. If we share God's holiness, our likeness mirrors God's holiness and love in all that we think and do.

We are linked to "God Supreme" through faith in Christ. Those who abide in Christ, says Wesley, are "fashioned like the God Supreme." Christ, the mediator, joins us to God the Father. Wesley stresses that we are fashioned like the divine—we bear God's image. "The image is thus a God-given potentiality for sharing in the divine life."[24]

Wesley's three-stanza interpretation of 2 Pet 1:4 reads like a poetical summary of the following interpretation of St. Cyril of Alexandria.

> In what way are we "partakers of the divine nature" (2 Pet 1:4)? We do not limit our boast merely to the fact that Christ wished to take us into an intimate relationship with him. No, the truth of the matter is evident to us all. For "the divine nature" is God the Word together with the flesh. And we are his "offspring" even though he is God by nature, on account of his taking the same flesh as ourselves. Therefore the mode of the relationship rests on likeness. For just as he is intimately related to the Father, and the

---

23. Hudson, *Becoming God*, 33–34.
24. Ibid., 74.

Father through the identity of the nature is intimately related to him, so we too are intimately related to him—in that he became man—and he to us. We are united to the Father through him as through a mediator. For Christ is, so to speak, a frontier between supreme divinity and humanity, since both are present within him. And containing within him, as it were, two such very different things, he is united on the one hand to God the Father, since he is God by nature, and on the other to human beings, since he is truly human.[25]

Our relationship to God is uniquely intimate since Christ the Mediator shares his being with God the Father and with us. This is a clear affirmation of St. Cyril of Alexandria and of Charles Wesley.

Trinity and the Image of God

In *Trinity Hymns* 1767 Wesley addresses further the matter of the image of God in a poem based on Gen 1:26, "And God said, Let us make man in our image, after our likeness."

> 1. Hail Father, Son, and Spirit, great
>   Before the birth of time,
> Enthroned in everlasting state
>   JEHOVAH ELOHIM!
> A mystical plurality
>   We in the Godhead own,
> Adoring One in Persons Three,
>   And Three in nature One.
>
> 2. From thee our being we receive
>   The creatures of thy grace,
> And raised out of the earth we live
>   To sing our Maker's praise:
> Thy powerful, wise, and loving mind
>   Did our creation plan,
> And all the glorious Persons joined
>   To form thy fav'rite, man.

---

25. *Commentary on John* 6.1, 653de; cited in Russell, *Fellow Workers with God*, 67–68.

3. Again thou didst, in council met,
>   Thy ruined work restore,
> Established in our first estate
>   To forfeit it no more:
> *And when we rise in love renewed,*
>   *Our souls resemble thee,*
> *An image of the Tri-une God*
>   *To all eternity.*[26]

The image of God has various interpretations in the writings of the early church fathers. Wesley claims in stanza 3 that the ability of human beings to "rise in love renewed" is the process whereby we resemble "an image of the Tri-une God." This interpretation is similar to that of the seventh-century monk St. John Climacus in his volume *Ladder of Divine Ascent*. The book is arranged in thirty parts or steps, one for each of the years of Christ's age at the time of his baptism. It addresses the path toward the highest degree of attainable spiritual perfection. In the final step, #30, he says, "Love, by reason of its nature, is a resemblance to God, as far as that is possible for mortals; in its activity it is inebriation of the soul; and by its distinctive property it is a fountain of faith, an abyss of patience, a sea of humility."[27]

---

26. *Trinity Hymns 1767*, 58, Hymn 87.
27. Climacus, *Ladder of Divine Ascent*, 127.

7

The Church and Participation in the Divine Nature

The Language of Personal and Corporate Participation

Charles Wesley often emphasizes personal deification. We read such lines in his poetry as

- Being of beings, make
  In me thy nature known.
- Thee, Saviour, I my refuge make;
  And when thy nature I partake.
- And make me all divine.
- Change my nature into thine,
  In me thy whole image shine.
- Heav'nly Adam, life divine,
  Change my nature into thine.
- Till of thy nature I partake,
  And bright in all thine image wake.
- Let all my soul become divine.
- Till I thy name, thy nature know.
- Transform my nature into thine.
  ...
  Let all my soul become divine.

Deification is unquestionably personal, as the above lines affirm, though it would be a gross error to read such lines in isolation. There follows an example in which within four lines of poetry Wesley uses both plural and singular pronouns to describe stamping the divine image, nature, and name on the human heart. In this instance *image, nature,* and *name* are used as synonyms.

> Our holiness, thyself impart,
>> Absorb whate'er is I in thine,
> And stamp the image on our heart,
>> The nature, and the name divine.[1]

What an eloquent line is "Absorb whate'er is I in thine"! What a superb description of personal participation in the divine nature! The "I," all that one is—all that embodies the individual—is absorbed into the divine nature.

As often as he uses the first person or personal emphasis Wesley also employs the plural. Hence, one reads such phrases or sentences as

- Thee let all our nature own.
- We participate of thine,
  Human nature of divine.
- Hear us, who thy nature share,
  Who thy mystic body are.
- Partakers of thy sacrifice,
  may we all thy nature share.
- And make us all divine.
- That we might partake
  The nature divine.
- And fill us with the life divine.
- Into all our souls impart,
  Thy divine unsinning nature.
- His nature, and his mind,
  He hath on us bestowed.
- Our nature too becomes divine,
  And God himself is man.
- And receive us as gods to a share of thy throne.

---

1. *Scripture Hymns* 1762, 2:289, Hymn 546:1b. The poem is based on 1 Cor 1:30, "Christ Jesus is made unto us wisdom, and righteousness, and sanctification, and redemption."

- Thy nature with our nature joined.
- Let every soul thy nature know.
- Thy nature doth itself impart
  To every humble, longing heart.
- Made like our Creator we gloriously shine,
  And bear the new nature the image divine.
- Thy nature we partake.
- Who makes in us his nature known.

Clearly, both the personal and corporate emphases have been taken out of their poetical contexts by placing the above lines simply in lists. It is not the purpose, however, to interpret them in isolation, but rather to illustrate both the personal and corporate dimensions of participation as expressed in Wesley's poetry.

The Ecclesial Context and the Eucharist

Wesley does not conceive of participation of an individual in the divine nature apart from the church, the body of Christ. He makes this very clear in a response to John 6:55–56, "My flesh is meat indeed, and my blood is drink indeed. He that eateth my flesh, and drinketh my blood, dwelleth in me, and I in him." He writes,

> Saviour, thy flesh is meat indeed!
> *Thy nature to thy church made known*
> Doth every saint with manna feed,
> *Till every saint with thee is one,*
> Till blended with its heavenly food
> The soul thy gracious fullness feels,
> And all transformed we dwell in God,
> And God in us forever dwells.[2]

This is unquestionably a eucharistic reference, though it does not come from the Wesleys' *HLS* 1745. In the opening sentence of the poem Charles reiterates the first line of the John passage: "Saviour, thy flesh is meat indeed!" This is the means whereby God makes the divine nature known to and experienced by the church. The eucharistic meal sustains "every saint"

---

2. Ibid., 2:248, Hymn 427. Italics added for emphasis.

and leads to full unity with God's nature: "Till every saint with thee is one." Wesley stresses that one experiences, one "feels," God's gracious fullness and is so transformed that there transpires a mutual "indwelling": "we dwell in God, / And God in us forever dwells." Hence, the "indwelling" is not merely intellectual assent, but rather a mutual divine/human experience. As I have written elsewhere,

> The church is also born of the Spirit, united in Christ, and in the Eucharist one experiences the "perfect harmony" of the church.
>
> Who thy mysterious supper share,
>   Here at thy table fed,
> Many, and yet but one we are,
>   One undivided Bread.[3]
>
> Wesley emphasizes the centrality of [participation] in the mystical body at the table. We are "one with the Living Bread Divine." Our hearts, minds, and spirits all meet and are joined in Jesus. As intimate as the bond in Christ may be on earth, however, it is but a foreshadowing of the close tie that shall bind the church eternal.[4]

Wesley's thoughts are in concert with St. John Chrysostom in reference to the unity of our natures with Christ, that is, with the entire constituency of the church.

> It is necessary to learn of the miracle of the Mysteries; what they are, why they were given, and what their benefits are. We become one body and members, the Scriptures say, of His body and of His bones. This takes place through the food which He has granted to us, desiring thus to show how much He cares for us. That is why He joined Himself with us and commingled His body with ours, so that we might be one, just as the body is joined to the head.[5]

In the eighteenth century the eucharistic nature of the church by no means dominated the ecclesial consciousness of the Church of England and its clergy. Charles Wesley laments,

---

3. *HLS* 1745, 138, Hymn 165:2; stanza 2 of a four-stanza hymn.
4. Kimbrough, "Charles Wesley's Understanding," 131–32.
5. Homily 46, PG 59, 260B.

> Why is the faithful seed decreased,
>> The life of God extinct and dead?
> The daily sacrifice is ceased,
>> And charity to heaven is fled.[6]

"The daily sacrifice" is a reference to Holy Communion. The practice of the early church Wesley describes in stanza 4:

> From house to house they broke the bread
>> *Impregnated with life divine,*
> And drank the Spirit of their Head
>> Transmitted in the sacred wine.[7]

The Wesley brothers and others (e.g., Nonjurors) who had a strong desire to return to the ecclesiology of the ancient church and its practices were an exception among eighteenth-century Anglican clergy. Unquestionably the joint publication, *HLS* 1745, of John and Charles Wesley emphasized the eucharistic shape of ecclesiology, even if the introduction to the volume did not spell this out. Knowingly or unknowingly, they pioneered a return to the eucharistic ecclesiology of the ancient church.

Charles Wesley's ecclesiology, though he does not use that word, is eucharistic and pneumatological. Just as the eucharistic meal identifies the uniqueness of the church and its mission, so do the presence and gifts of the Holy Spirit. It is not a coincidence that early in *HLS* 1745 one encounters a powerful hymn to the Holy Spirit.

> 1. Come, thou everlasting Spirit,
>> Bring to every thankful mind
> All the Saviour's dying merit
>> All his suffering for mankind:
> True recorder of his passion,
>> Now the living faith impart,
> Now reveal his great salvation,
>> Preach his gospel to our heart.

---

6. *HLS* 1745, 140, Hymn 156:11; stanza 11 of a twenty-two stanza poem.
7. Ibid., 139, Hymn 156:4; stanza 4 of the poem just cited.

> 2. Come, thou witness of his dying,
>   Come, remembrancer divine,
> Let us feel thy power applying
>   Christ to every soul and mine;
> Let us groan thine inward groaning,
>   Look on him we pierced, and grieve,
> All receive the grace atoning,
>   All the sprinkled blood receive.[8]

Charles Wesley is clear about the soteriological functions of the Holy Spirit: it awakens the mind to the merits of the Savior's suffering and death; it imparts living faith, reveals salvation, and proclaims the gospel to human hearts. The Holy Spirit is the means whereby we *feel* the power of Christ applied to our souls and we receive atoning grace.

In exploring Charles Wesley's understanding of deification and the church it is vital to understand that he has a eucharistic and Trinitarian approach to all dimensions of theology. The focus on eucharistic theology emphasizes that local communities are of foremost importance and the context in which Christians live out their faith. Trinitarian theology focuses on God's internal life of communion and God's salvation history, and it seeks to embrace all creation in this divine communion. Deification poses the lifelong question for all Christians and the church: How do we share in the communion that is present in the Trinity? This is a question Wesley is ever asking.

Wesley takes great care to emphasize the corporate unity of the fellowship of believers, namely, the church, in the following text from *HLS* 1745.

> 2. With him the Corner Stone
>   The living stones conjoin,
> Christ and his Church are One,
>   One body and one vine,
> For us he uses all his powers,
> And all he has, or is, is ours.[9]

"The living stones" are the people of God in the church, and in Christ the church is one with God and one another; and all that is Christ's, "all He has, or is, is Ours," that is, the members of the body, the church.

---

8. Ibid., 13, Hymn 16.
9. Ibid., 110, Hymn 129:2; stanza 2 of a three-stanza hymn.

Wesley's emphasis on the unity of the body of Christ reminds one of St. John Chrysostom's metaphor of the wheat in speaking of the unity of the church.

> Just as the bread is constituted by many grains united together so that the grains cannot be distinguished from one another even though they are there, since their difference is made unapparent in their cohesion, in the same manner we are joined together both to each other and to Christ. For you are not part of one body, and your neighbor part of another, but all are part of the same body. For this reason, he [St. Paul] emphasizes "all of us partake of one bread" (1 Corinthinans 10:17).[10]

Unity of the Mystic Body

In Part 1 of a lengthy poem titled "The Communion of Saints,"[11] the corporate unity of the church is eloquently underscored by Wesley. The root of such unity is in the Holy Trinity, to which one is mystically joined, as the Father, Son, and Spirit are joined as one. The unity is so strong that the Trinity is to own human nature: "Thee let all our nature own, / One in Three, and Three in One."

> 1. Father, Son, and Spirit, hear
> Faith's effectual, fervent prayer.
> Hear and our petitions seal;
> Let us now the answer feel.
>
> Mystically one with thee,
> Transcript of the Trinity,
> Thee let all our nature own,
> One in Three, and Three in One.

Stanza 2 emphasizes the ever-increasing strength of the bond of unity. It is not enough, avers Wesley, that sins have been forgiven and one is an inheritor of eternal life; the church is always in need of a strengthened bond of fellowship and peace. It must not cease to pray: "Join our new-born spirits, join / each to each, and all to thine."

---

10. Homily 24 on First Corinthians, PG 61, 200.
11. *HSP* 1740, 188–90, Part 1, stanzas 1–3 of a seven-stanza poem appear here.

The Church and Participation

   2. If we now begin to be
      Partners with thy saints and thee,
      If we have our sins forgiven,
      Fellow-citizens of heaven,

      Still the fellowship increase,
      Knit us in the bond of peace,
      Join our new-born spirits, join
      Each to each, and all to thine.

Stanza 3 is a prayer that epitomizes what the church should be. Wesley is keenly aware of the fragmented church of the eighteenth century. The church cannot be what human beings wish to make of it. It is God's. The hope of the "one high calling" is this: one Spirit, one baptism, one faith, one Father "over, through, and in us all." Even if we think we have grasped this reality about the church, humility brings us to our knees with the affirmation "God incomprehensible."

   3. Build us in one body up,
      Called in one high calling's hope;
      One the Spirit whom we claim,
      One the pure baptismal flame,

      One the faith, and common Lord,
      One the Father lives, adored
      Over, through, and in us all,
      God incomprehensible.

In Part 4 of the same poem[12] Wesley explores in a prayer the meaning of the "oneness" or "unity" of those "who thy mystic body are," who share the divine nature, namely, the church.

   1. Christ, from whom all blessings flow,
      Perfecting the saints below,
      Hear us, who thy nature share,
      Who thy mystic body are:

---

12. Ibid., 194–95, Part 4:1–5. All five stanzas of the poem appear here.

> Join us, in one spirit, join,
> Let us still receive of thine,
> Still for more on thee we call,
> Thee, who fillest all in all.

The realities of unity for which Wesley prays mirror the deified church of Christ. That for which he prays is what the deified church should be. In stanza 1 the supplication "Join us, in one spirit, join" is what the members of the body are to be—joined in one spirit. Nevertheless, even if so joined, "Still for more on thee we call." In stanza 2 he expands the "more" of which he speaks.

Merely to be joined in one spirit is insufficient, hence, in stanza 2 Wesley pleads that the church will be "closer knit to thee our head."

> 2. Closer knit to thee our head,
>   Nourish us, O Christ, and feed,
>   Let us daily growth receive,
>   More and more in Jesus live:
>
>   Jesu! We thy members are,
>   Cherish us with kindest care,
>   Of thy flesh, and of thy bone:
>   Love, forever love thine own.

Stagnant unity is not an option. Growth in unity with Christ is an ongoing process of daily nurture. One is never so closely knit to Christ that further growth is unnecessary. One must "more and more in Jesus live." The intimacy of this relationship he describes as "of thy flesh, and of thy bone"[13] expressed through an eternal love.

The series of verbs (*move, actuate, guide, divide*) used in stanza 3 are vital to a united, deified church.

> 3. Move, and actuate, and guide,
>   Diverse gifts to each divide;
>   Placed according to thy will,
>   Let us all our work fulfill,

---

13. See Gen 2:23.

The Church and Participation

> Never from our office move,
> Needful to the others prove,
> Use the grace on each bestowed,
> Tempered by the art of God.

Wesley prays for a church that is moved, guided, and motivated to fulfill God's will with the diverse gifts with which the members have been divinely endowed.

The members of Christ's body are to be mutually needful to one another and blessed to use the grace that has been bestowed upon them. Then comes his eloquent, and perhaps elusive, phrase "Tempered by the art of God." It suggests that as one uses divine grace in relationships one practices the art of balance, which is a difficult art, but vital to a community with diverse gifts and with members' wills that somehow must be brought into congruence with divine will.

The Deified Church

In stanza 4 Wesley describes in part how the deified church, which shares God's nature, lives, that is, how it behaves.

> 4. Sweetly now we all agree,
> Touched with softest sympathy,
> Kindly for each other care:
> Every member feels its share:
>
> Wounded by the grief of one,
> All the suffering members groan;
> Honoured if one member is
> All partake the common bliss.

No doubt these lines express the ideal of the deified church, rather than its reality: all sweetly agree and are touched by softest sympathy; they kindly care for each other, and "every member feels its share." When one member grieves all mutually grieve, and when one member is honored all share in common joy. This is hardly a description of the Christian church as history reveals it, for it is often marked by discord, strife, contempt, and even violence.

In stanza 5 Wesley provides the crowning description of the deified church.

5. Many are we now, and one,
   We who Jesus have put on:
   There is neither bond nor free,
   Male nor female, Lord, in thee.

   Love, like death, hath all destroyed,
   Rendered all distinctions void:
   Names, and sects, and parties fall;
   Thou, O Christ, art ALL in ALL!

The oneness of the body of Christ transcends all distinction. He uses the terms *bond* and *free*, which had distinct meaning in the eighteenth century, for men and women were sold into slavery at that time. During the years he made his home in Bristol he most certainly knew of the slave ships that docked and departed from there.[14] The distinctions of male and female were also of particular significance in this century, since women were gravely suppressed with little or no education, except among the aristocracy, and in many other facets of society. To say then that the body of Christ, the church, has a unity that transcends all distinctions is quite daring. Nevertheless, Charles Wesley is not saying distinctions are nonexistent, but rather that the love of Christ renders them void. In a country that had experienced the break with the Roman Church under King Henry VIII and was filled with a plethora of Protestant dissenting groups and sects, as well as diverse political parties, it is indeed significant, if not revolutionary, to aver that "names, and sects, and parties fall." Yet, Wesley is not saying this for its revolutionary or political value in an ecclesial or secular realm; rather, he is outlining the identity and ultimate goal of the deified church. Such oneness and mutual caring is the body of Christ that shares in the nature of God. St. Symeon the New Theologian declares, "He became totally man, He truly and completely God . . . and the same One is completely God in the totality of His members."[15]

These are they *"who thy nature share, / Who thy mystic body are,"* as Wesley says in stanza 1, Part 1 of the poem.

---

14. There is a fascinating exchange of letters between Charles Wesley and two former African slaves, Ephraim Robin John and Ancona Robin John, who studied English briefly under Wesley in Bristol. He nurtured them as well in the Christian faith. See Kimbrough, "Charles Wesley and Slavery."

15. *Hymn* 15, 204, quoted in Golitzin, *On the Mystical Life*, 3:91.

The Church and Participation
Unity through the Eucharist

Wesley further emphasizes God's incomprehensibility and the mystery of deification. How unity comes to the church in and through the Eucharist, how the divine nature is imparted to the faithful through the bread and wine remains a mystery. He asks,

> 1. O the depth of Love Divine,
> Th' unfathomable grace!
> Who shall say how bread and wine
> God into man conveys?
> *How* the bread his faith imparts,
> *How* the wine transmits his blood,
> Fills his faithful peoples' hearts
> With all the life of God![16]

The quest to grasp the significance and meaning of this "Love Divine" that comes into every life through the bread and wine is lifelong. We may not understand how we become one as the body of Christ and with Christ in the Eucharist, but we can experience the mystery and the reality.

> 1. How happy are thy servants, Lord,
> Who thus remember thee!
> What tongue can tell our sweet accord,
> Our perfect harmony!
>
> 2. Who thy Mysterious Supper share,
> Here at thy table fed,
> Many, and yet but One we are,
> One undivided Bread.
>
> 3. *One with the Living Bread Divine,*
> Which now by faith we eat,
> Our hearts, and minds, and spirits join,
> And all in Jesus meet.[17]

---

16. *HLS* 1745, 41, Hymn 57:1; stanza 1 of a four-stanza hymn.

17. Ibid., 138, Hymn 165:1–3; stanzas 1–3 of a four-stanza hymn. Italics added for emphasis.

What Norman Russell affirms for Orthodoxy is valid for Charles Wesley's theology as well. "We cannot achieve theosis on our own. We need ecclesial community in which we are re-created in the image of God through baptism and the Eucharist."[18] "The Church alone is the place of Theosis."[19] This is unequivocally so for Charles Wesley, for as he told the Society at Rotherham, "there was no salvation *out of the church*; that is, out of the mystical body of Christ, or the company of faithful people."[20]

---

18. Russell, *Fellow Workers with God*, 41.
19. Archimandrite George, *Theosis*, 36.
20. *MSJ*, 2:625.

8

Divine Love and Participation in the Divine Nature

The end of the creation of humankind is the love of God. In his brother John's sermon "The One Thing Needful," which Charles preached a number of times, love is affirmed as the key to human existence, for "by love man is not only made like God, but in some sense one with him." The sermon states emphatically, "love is the very image of God."

> 2. Now, that the recovery of the image of God, of this glorious liberty, of this perfect soundness, is the one thing needful upon earth, appears first from hence, that the enjoyment of them was the one end of our creation. For to this end was man created, to love God; and to this end alone, even to love the Lord his God with all his heart, soul, mind, and strength. But love is the very image of God: it is the brightness of his glory. *By love man is not only made like God, but in some sense one with him.* "*If any man love God, God loveth him, and cometh to him, and maketh his abode with him*' [cf. John 14:23]. *He "dwelleth in God, and God in him*" [cf. 1 John 4:12, 15, 16]; *and "he that is thus joined to the Lord is one spirit*" [cf. 1 Cor 6:17].[1] Love is perfect freedom; as there is no fear, or pain, so there is no constraint in love. Whoever acts from this principle alone, he doth whatsoever he will. All his thoughts move freely; they follow the bent of his own mind, they run after the beloved object. All his words flow easy and unconstrained; for it is the abundance of the heart that dictates. All his actions are the result of pure choice: the thing he would, that he does, and that only. Love is the health of the soul, the full exertion of all its powers, the perfection of all its faculties. Therefore, since the enjoyment of these was the one end of our creation, the recovering of them is the one thing now needful.[2]

1. Italics added for emphasis.
2. Wesley, *Sermons*, 365.

Love—the Nature of God

One cannot understand Charles Wesley's concept of participation in the divine nature without grasping the important role love plays in joining the human and divine. As this sermon asserts, "Love is the health of the soul, the full exertion of all its powers, the perfection of all its faculties." Love enables the reciprocal indwelling of God and humankind. Through such love one is "joined to the Lord in one spirit."

There is perhaps no more dominant theme in the writings of Charles Wesley as relates to God's nature than "love," for, as Scripture states, "God is love" (1 John 4:8). In one of his most highly praised poems, "Wrestling Jacob,"[3] known to many by its first line "Come, O thou Traveller unknown," there is a refrain that occurs four times: "Thy nature, and thy name is love." The poem is based on Gen 32:24–32 (KJV):

> And Jacob was left alone; and there wrestled a man with him until the breaking of the day. And when he saw that he prevailed not against him, he touched the hollow of his thigh; and the hollow of Jacob's thigh was out of joint, as he wrestled with him. And he said, Let me go, for the day breaketh. And he said, I will not let thee go, except thou bless me. And he said unto him, What is thy name? And he said, Jacob. And he said, Thy name shall be called no more Jacob, but Israel: for as a prince hast thou power with God and with men, and hast prevailed. And Jacob asked him, and said, Tell me, I pray thee, thy name. And he said, Wherefore is it that thou dost ask after my name? And he blessed him there. And Jacob called the name of the place Peniel: for I have seen God face to face, and my life is preserved. And as he passed over Penuel the sun rose upon him, and he halted upon his thigh. Therefore the children of Israel eat not of the sinew which shrank, which is upon the hollow of the thigh, unto this day: because he touched the hollow of Jacob's thigh in the sinew that shrank.

> 1. Come, O thou Traveller unknown,
>   Whom still I hold, but cannot see!
> My company before is gone,
>   And I am left alone with thee;
> With thee all night I mean to stay
> And wrestle till the break of day.

---

3. *HSP* 1742, 115–18. The original poem includes fourteen stanzas.

Divine Love and Participation

2. I need not tell thee who I am,
    My misery or sin declare;
Thyself hast called me by my name,
    Look on thy hands and read it there.
But who, I ask thee, who art thou?
Tell me thy name, and tell me now.

3. In vain thou strugglest to get free,
    I never will unloose my hold;
Art thou the man that died for me?
    The secret of thy love unfold;
Wrestling, I will not let thee go
Till I thy name, thy nature know.[4]

4. Wilt thou not yet to me reveal
    Thy new, unutterable name?
Tell me, I still beseech thee, tell,
    To know it now resolved I am;
Wrestling, I will not let thee go
Till I thy name, thy nature know.

5. 'Tis all in vain to hold thy tongue
    Or touch the hollow of my thigh;
Though every sinew be unstrung,
    Out of my arms thou shalt not fly;
Wrestling I will not let thee go
Till I thy name, thy nature know.

6. What though my shrinking flesh complain
    And murmur to contend so long?
I rise superior to my pain:
    When I am weak then I am strong,
And when my all of strength shall fail
I shall with the God-man prevail.

---

4. Italics throughout the poem are added for emphasis.

7. My strength is gone, my nature dies,
        I sink beneath thy weighty hand,
Faint to revive, and fall to rise;
        I fall, and yet by faith I stand;
I stand and will not let thee go
Till I thy name, thy nature know.

8. Yield to me now—for I am weak
        But confident in self-despair!
Speak to my heart, in blessing speak,
        Be conquered by my instant prayer:
Speak, or thou never hence shalt move,
And tell me if thy name is Love.

9. 'Tis Love! 'tis Love! thou diedst for me,
        I hear thy whisper in my heart.
The morning breaks, the shadows flee,
        Pure Universal Love thou art:
To me, to all, thy mercies move—
Thy nature, and thy name is Love.

10. My prayer hath power with God; the grace
        Unspeakable I now receive;
Through faith I see thee face to face,
        I see thee face to face, and live!
In vain I have not wept and strove—
Thy nature, and thy name is Love.

11. I know thee, Saviour, who thou art,
        Jesus, the feeble sinner's friend;
Nor wilt thou with the night depart,
        But stay and love me to the end:
Thy mercies never shall remove,
Thy nature, and thy name is Love.

12. The Sun of Righteousness on me
    Hath risen with healing in his wings:
Withered my nature's strength; from thee
    My soul its life and succor brings;
My help is all laid up above;
Thy nature, and thy name is Love.

13. Contented now upon my thigh
    I halt, till life's short journey end;
All helplessness, all weakness I
    On thee alone for strength depend;
Nor have I power from thee to move:
Thy nature, and thy name is Love.

14. Lame as I am, I take the prey,
    Hell, earth, and sin with ease overcome;
I leap for joy, pursue my way,
    And as a bounding hart fly home,
Through all eternity to prove
Thy nature, and thy name is Love.

Wesley uses Jacob's wrestling with the angel as a metaphor for the human struggle to comprehend God's nature. He sees the lives of all people mirrored in Jacob's struggle with the angel. This is the human struggle of the ages, that is, the quest to know the name and nature of God. We grasp for the unknown and hold fast to that which is a mystery. Stanzas 1 through 6 tell of the agony of the struggle, the mental and physical pain, and the soul-searching questions, which often drive many away from God. Stanzas 7 through 14, however, describe the discovery of faith, which resounds in the refrain: "Thy nature, and thy name is Love." Love is who God is; love is what God is like; and love is the way in which God's self-disclosure is revealed. It is God's love made known in Jesus that makes the shadows of doubt flee as dawn breaks and one confesses, "Pure, universal Love thou art!"

For Charles Wesley love is the key to participation in the divine nature, for God's nature is love. He understands as did St. Irenaeus that God "in his immense love . . . became what we are, that he might make us what he is."⁵ How is this realized among the faithful? Dimitar Kirov avers, "Through love of God one becomes Godlike and participates in *theosis* or deification."⁶

Transformation in Love

The equation of God's nature with love is a rather constant theme of Wesley's poetry. He knows that only if one can be transformed into love can one experience the indwelling of God's nature. It is not enough to be changed into divine love at death; Wesley anticipates such a change in this life. He writes,

> 2. Death I no more desire
> >   By countless woes opprest;
> Do thou my soul require,
> >   Whene'er thou know'st it best:
> Sooner, O God, or later
> >   My soul from earth remove,
> *But first impart thy nature,*
> >   *And change me into love.*⁷

These lines, published in 1767, are consistent with the last stanza of Wesley's well-known hymn, "O for a heart to praise my God," which appeared twenty-five years earlier in *HSP* 1742. Once more he stresses the imparting of God's nature so that God's name of love will be written in the heart. In the above stanza he emphasizes the need for such transformation in the present.

> 8. *Thy nature, dearest Lord, impart,*
> >   Come quickly from above,
> Write thy new name upon my heart,
> >   *Thy new, best name of love.*⁸

---

5. Irenaeus, *Adversus Haereses*, 5. praef.

6. Kirov, "Unity of Revelation," 109.

7. *Family Hymns* 1767, 101, Hymn 95:2; stanza 2 of a two-stanza hymn. Italics added for emphasis.

8. *HSP* 1742, 31, stanza 8 of an eight-stanza hymn based on Ps 51:10: "Make me a clean heart, O God, and renew a right spirit within me" (BCP). Italics added for emphasis.

Divine Love and Participation

God's nature, being love, begets love. Divine love begetting divine love is an essential part of the soteriological process: "His nature pure, his love imparts."

> 1. The voice of God the Father sounds
>   Salvation to our sinful race:
> His grace above our sin abounds,
>   His glory shines in Jesus' face,
> And by the Person of the Son
> The Father makes salvation known.
>
> 2. Saved by the Son, the Lord our God
>   Jehovah's fellow we proclaim,
> Who washes us in his own blood,
>   To us declares his Father's name,
> *His nature pure, his love imparts,*
> With all his fullness to our hearts.[9]

Here Wesley emphasizes the christocentric focus of divine love. It is self-giving and sacrificial love embodied in the "Person of the Son" through whom God the Father makes salvation known. Once again it is an indwelling love that is to fill our hearts completely. How can this be when there are many forces within and without human beings vying for allegiance? Wesley is keenly aware of this reality and offers a prayer in the last four lines of the following stanza from *Family Hymns* 1767, which should be the constant prayer of all believers.

> 3.   With resigned simplicity
>   And patient earnestness,
>   Thee we seek; not thine, but thee
>   We languish to possess:
>   *Come, and bring thy nature in,*
>   *And let thy love unrivaled reign;*
>   *Grace we then, and glory win,*
>   *And all in Jesus gain.*[10]

---

9. *Trinity Hymns* 1767, 8, Hymn 8. The poem is based on Hos 1:7, "I will have mercy upon the house of Judah, and will save them by the LORD their God."

10. *Family Hymns* 1767, 30, Hymn 28:3; stanza 3 of a three-stanza hymn. Italics added for emphasis.

The rival forces within are very real to Wesley. Throughout his life he struggles with many of them. In the quest for the realization of perfect love in his life he knows there are obstacles all along the way. There are torturing passions that must be removed.

> 2. Jesus, thy gracious nature tell,
>   Thy saving name in me reveal,
>   The tort'ring passion to remove,
>   T' expel what now thou dost control,
>   *Thy nature speak into my soul*
>   Thy favorite name of perfect love.[11]

What is the saving name that can remove such passion and expel other threatening forces? It is God's name of "perfect love," which must be integrated into the human soul. St. Isaac the Syrian says, "When one obtains love, he[/she] is, together with it, clothed in God."[12] In other words, as Wesley says, perfect love has filled the soul.

Gradual Deification through Divine Love

Participation in God's nature is not a stagnant state. It is an ongoing process throughout one's life. In the pursuit of perfect love the Christian cannot simply say, "I have arrived. I am perfected. I have the full nature of God within." Here Wesley is perhaps close to Origen, St. Ephrem the Syrian, and St. Gregory of Nyssa, who see the deification process as gradual. Therefore, one constantly pleads, "Come, and bring thy nature in, / And let thy love unrivaled reign." This is the reason Wesley prays,

> 3. Yet I in my lost condition
>   May approach the sinner's friend,
>   Still presenting my petition,
>   Saviour, in the cloud descend:
>   Make thy goodness pass before me,
>   God discovered from above,
>   *To thine image here restore me,*
>   *Change my nature into love.*[13]

---

11. *Scripture Hymns* 1762, 2:71, Hymn 1325:2; stanza 2 of a two-stanza hymn based on Hos 12:4, "He had power over the angel, and prevailed: he wept, and made supplication unto him." Italics added for emphasis.

12. *Logos* 91, "Concerning the Distinctions of Virtues," 308.

13. *Preparation for Death* 1772, 40, Hymn 37:3; stanza 3 of a five-stanza hymn. Italics added for emphasis.

Divine Love and Participation

Wesley's last two lines do not say, "To thine image you've restored me, / Changed my nature into love." He knows the transformation is a gradual process.

The anticipation of human nature transformed into love through the restoration of the divine image is a very real possibility for Wesley. While it is the divine initiative to change one's nature into love, a human response is also requisite. Thus he writes,

> 2. Thy hands shall never more hang down,
>   Jehovah bids thy fears depart;
> Jehovah is thy shield and sun,
>   Fixt in the center of thy heart:
> Diffusing thence his heat and light
> *He bids thee all his nature prove,*
> *And comprehend the depth and height,*
> *And length and breadth of Jesu's love.*[14]

What does he mean by "He bids thee all his nature prove"? In the process toward deification one affirms God's nature in one's life by comprehending "the depth and height, / And length and breadth of Jesu's love." This is not an instantaneous occurrence. It is a lifelong process.

While the transformation of human nature in deification involves the indwelling of God's nature, love, in the human soul and spirit, such transformation has an outward visibility. It does not remain hidden. The outward appearance of participation is by no means for human gratification; it has a salvific purpose.

> 15. Thy gracious readiness
>   To save mankind assert,
> Thine image, love, thy name impress,
>   *Thy nature on my heart.*
>   Bowels of mercy, hear,
>   Into my soul come down,
> *Let it throughout my life appear*
> *That I have Christ put on.*[15]

---

14. *Scripture Hymns* 1762, 2:97, Hymn 1397:2; stanza 2 of a two-stanza hymn based on Zeph 3:14–15, "Sing, O daughter of Zion; shout, O Israel; be glad and rejoice with all the heart, O daughter of Jerusalem. The LORD hath taken away thy judgments, he hath cast out thine enemy: the king of Israel, even the LORD, is in the midst of thee: thou shalt not see evil any more."

15. *HGEL* 1742, 50, Hymn 16:15; stanza 15 of a sixteen-stanza hymn based on 1

Visibility of God's Divine Nature—Love

Deification results in the visibility of the nature of God, namely, love. Wesley uses the language of dressing, that is, putting on one's clothes, when he says that one's appearance will reflect having "Christ put on."[16] Again, this is part of God's saving process. There is an evangelistic witness in putting on Christ. This is part of the "gracious readiness . . . to save mankind" of which Wesley speaks in the previous poem. What is the garment that we have put on when we put on Christ? The garment of God's nature, love.

This leads then to a discussion of love's active role in the Christian's life. While God's nature, love, dwells within, it is a dynamic force in the life of the Christian, the church, and the community. Love is not passive; it is a force for good and redemption. It changes things. In some perhaps more familiar words Wesley affirms,

> 5. Many are we now, and one,
> We who Jesus have put on:
> There is neither bond nor free,
> Male nor female, Lord, in thee.
>
> Love, like death, hath all destroyed,
> Rendered all distinctions void:
> Names, and sects, and parties fall;
> Thou, O Christ, art ALL in ALL![17]

He uses again the metaphor of clothing oneself with Christ: "We who Jesus have put on." What happens when one is clothed with love? Unity transpires. Love renders "all distinctions void." This is the result of participating in God's nature, for love actively *renders*, in other words it engages "all distinctions" and nullifies them! Since there is a christocentric focus for all of life, one is not preoccupied with the labels of names, particular sects and parties. Christ has become "ALL in ALL." Once again, this is how the nature of God in human beings changes the church, community, and world. Divine love transforms all followers of Christ into divine love, which is then ever present. According to Demetrios L. Stathopoulos, St. Symeon

---

Timothy 2:4: "God will have ALL men to be saved." Italics added for emphasis.

16. See Rom 3:27 and 13:14.

17. *HSP* 1740, 195, stanza 5 of Part IV of the poem titled "The Communion of Saints."

the New Theologian views love as "not merely an attribute of God, but the substantial presence of God."[18]

Active Love

The active engagement of love is eloquently expressed by Charles Wesley in lines selected by this author to shape the hymn "Come, O holy God and true" from a 162-line poem titled "The Beatitudes," which is based on Matt 5:3–12.[19]

> 1. Come, O holy God and true!
>   Come, and my whole heart renew;
>   Take me now, possess me whole,
>   Form the Saviour in my soul:
>
> REFRAIN:
> *Love immense, and unconfined,*
> *Love to all of humankind.*
>
> 2. In my heart thy name reveal,
>   Stamp me with thy Spirit's seal,
>   *Change my nature into thine,*
>   *In me thy whole image shine:*

Stanzas 1 and 2 are the prologue to the activities of love that Wesley describes in the remaining stanzas. They are the constant prayer he is ever praying: "possess me whole, form the Saviour in my soul"—in other words, possess me completely with divine love. Form the Savior, whose nature is love, in my soul. Then comes Wesley's familiar language in stanza 2: "change my nature into thine" in such a way that it is not confined within but has a bright appearance—the unmistakable appearance of divine love.

Wesley often speaks of being sealed by the Spirit. In one of the baptismal hymns already discussed there is the line "Annex your hallowing

---

18. Quoted in Golitzin, *On the Mystical Life*, 3:77.

19. *HSP* 1749, 1:38–39, No. 8: stanzas 1–2 = lines 97–104, stanzas 3–6 = lines 129–44; stanza 7 = lines 115–18; refrain = lines 113–14. Italics added for emphasis. "Come thou holy God and true" is a composite hymn created by S T Kimbrough, Jr., from the lines of the poem listed here. The composite hymn was first published in Kimbrough, *Songs for the Poor*.

Spirit's seal." In stanza 2 above he says, "Stamp me with your Spirit's seal." He uses similar language in speaking of "an inward baptism . . . of fire."

> 3. Transform my nature into thine,
>   Let all my powers thine impress feel,
>   Let all my soul become divine,
>   And stamp me with thy Spirit's seal.[20]

In the Eastern Church being sealed by the Spirit often refers to the gift of the Holy Spirit as the seal or *shragis*, connected with unction or *chrisma*, the anointing of oil. Wesley's language seems quite compatible with this liturgical act, though this is not its intention.

In stanza 3 Wesley specifically identifies divine love as "active love," which "emulates the Blessed above." Therefore, God's love is active and should be seen in every human action. Its radiance is such that it sparkles from within the soul.

> 3. Happy soul, whose active love
>   Emulates the Blessed above,
>   In thy every action seen,
>   Sparkling from the soul within:

There follows in stanzas 4 through 6 a quasi-litany of active love. As the selected refrain says, "Love immense, and unconfined, / Love to all of humankind." Because of the inclusive nature of active, divine love, it goes in search of all who suffer: the distressed widow, the poor and homeless, the sick and hungry, prisoners and the weak. Those who wander in darkness are brought into the light.

> 4. Thou to every sufferer nigh,
>   Hearest not in vain the cry
>   Of the widow in distress,
>   Of the poor, the fatherless:

> 5. Raiment thou to all that need,
>   To the hungry deal'st thy bread,
>   To the sick thou giv'st relief,
>   Sooth'st the hapless prisoner's grief.

---

20. *HSP* 1742, 136. The poem is based on Luke 12:50, "I have a baptism to be baptized with; and how I am straitened till it be accomplished!"

6. The weak hands thou liftest up,
   Bid'st the helpless mourners hope,
   Giv'st to those in darkness light,
   Guid'st the weary wanderers right.

What is there about the quality of this love that is unquestionably divine love, God's nature? Wesley describes it thus:

7. Love, which willeth all should live,
   Love, which all to all would give,
   Love, that over all prevails,
   Love, that never, never fails.

What a phenomenal description of God's nature! As human beings emulate these qualities and activities of love their own natures and those of others are transformed into God's nature. Love of God and love of neighbor are identical. This is love "which all to all would give."

Paradigms of Love

Once again Charles Wesley's theology is very close to Maximus the Confessor, who says that we do not divisively assign "one form of love to God and another to human beings, for it is one and the same and universal: owed to God and attaching human beings to one another. For the activity and proof of perfect love towards God is genuine disposition of goodwill toward one's neighbor (I John 4:20)."[21] Thus, it is not surprising that "St. John Chrysostom insisted that church members' behavior was the only effective missionary method."[22]

Deification is vital for all humankind, for "the divine-human reciprocity is love itself, the proper mode of existence in the world."[23]

Maximus also declares, "God and man are paradigms of one another, that as much as God is humanized to man through love for mankind, so much has man been able to deify himself to God through love."[24] Wesley's wording of the last part of this statement might read somewhat differently: "so much has man been able to partake of the divine nature through love." He uses the verb *deify* only once in all of his poetry. It occurs in stanza 7 of

---

21. Letter 2: On Love, quoted in Louth, *Maximus the Confessor*, 90.
22. Vassiliadis, *Eucharist and Witness*, 43.
23. Hudson, *Becoming God*, 34.
24. *Ambigua*, 10. See Russell, *Fellow Workers with God*, 39.

a nine-stanza poem published in *Funeral Hymns* 1759, which celebrates life beyond death. Of those who have passed beyond the grave into the divine presence he says, in the "world of spirits bright," as they worship the Holy Trinity, "They drink the *deifying* stream."

> 6. I see a world of spirits bright,
>   Who reap the pleasures there;
> They all are robed in purest white,
>   And conquering palms they bear:
> Adorned by their Redeemer's grace
>   They close pursue the Lamb,
> And every shining front displays
>   Th' unutterable name.
>
> 7. They drink the *deifying* stream,
>   They pluck th' ambrosial fruit,
> And each records the praise of him
>   Who tuned his golden lute:
> At once they strike th' harmonious wire,
>   And hymn the great Three-One:
> He hears; he smiles: and all the quire
>   Fall down before his throne.[25]

---

25. *Funeral Hymns* 1759, 5–6, Hymn 3:6–7; stanzas 6 and 7 of a nine-stanza hymn. Italics added for emphasis. An earlier version of the poem appears in MS Richmond, 136–39.

9

Illumination and Participation in the Divine Nature

IN THE PROGRESSION TOWARD deification, divine illumination in Orthodoxy is considered to be a higher stage in this sacred journey. God enables the faithful to view the world and humankind through the eyes of divine grace. One is overcome with the love of God, the world, and others.

Light from God the Creator

For Charles Wesley the origin of the illumination that accompanies sharing in God's nature has its roots in God the creator. In the following couplet from a two-stanza poem based on Isa 31:9, "The Lord's fire is in Sion, and his furnace in Jerusalem," he makes this quite clear:

> Made like our Creator we gloriously shine,
> And bear the new nature the image divine.[1]

In his *Hymn* 30, St. Symeon the New Theologian sings of the light whereby one is illumined within by God.

> I see Him within . . .
> suddenly become manifest,
> both united inexpressibly
> and ineffably joined
> and mingled with me unmingledly
> like fire with iron itself
> the light within a crystal,
> and He has made me like fire
> . . . like light.[2]

1. *Scripture Hymns* 1762, 1:328, Hymn 1016:2, lines 3–4.
2. St. Symeon, *Hymns of Divine Love*, lines 421–30, 168.

One is keenly aware of the inner illumination that is outwardly expressed. Wesley describes this phenomenon similarly.

> 3. Write upon me the name divine,
> *And let the Father's nature shine,*
> His image visibly exprest,
> His glory pouring from my breast
> O'er all my bright humanity,
> *Transformed into the God I see!*[3]

By saying, "And let the Father's nature shine . . . O'er all my bright humanity," Wesley affirms that we "participate in the divine brightness."[4] The biblical parallels of the transfiguration of Peter on Mount Tabor (Matt 17:4) and Moses' transfiguration on Sinai (Exod 34:30) emphasize the illumination of the human countenance, which transpires through divine revelation.

Individual and Corporate Illumination

Divine illumination, however, is not simply an individual matter. It pervades the entire church. In the poem "Lo, the church with gradual light," Wesley uses the metaphor of the moon to describe how the church, reflecting divine light, at times glows brightly with its borrowed rays, while at others the light is in full decline or in a long eclipse. The eschatological hope of the church is that Christ will drive away all diminished divine light and bring the perfect day when she "blazes with meridian light." Thus, the church shall shine forever brightly with the "light of truth divine, / And all the fire of love."

> 1. Lo, the church with gradual light
>   Her opening charms displays,
>   After a long dreary night
>   Looks forth with glimmering rays,

---

3. *Scripture Hymns* 1762, 2:421, Hymn 842:3. Italics added for emphasis. The five-stanza poem is based on Rev 3:12: "Him that overcometh will I make a pillar in the temple of my God, and he shall go no more out: and I will write upon him the name of my God, and the name of the city of my God, which is new Jerusalem, which cometh down out of heaven from my God: and I will write upon him my new name."

4. Macarios of Philadelphia, in Nicodemos of the Holy Mountain, *Handbook of Spiritual Counsel*, 224.

>   Scarce perceptible appears,
> Until the Day-spring from on high
>   All the face of nature cheers,
>   And gladdens earth and sky.
>
> 2.   Fair as the unclouded moon,
>   With borrowed rays she shines,
>   Shines, but ah! She changes soon,
>   And when at full declines,
>   Frequent, long eclipses feels,
> 'Till Jesus drives the shades away,
>   All her doubts and sins dispels,
>   And brings the perfect day.
>
> 3.   Now she without spot appears,
>   For Christ appears again,
>   Sun of righteousness, he clears
>   His church from every stain,
>   Rising in full majesty
> He blazes with meridian light:
>   All th' horizon laughs to see
>   The joyous heavenly sight.
>
> 4.   Bright with lustre not her own
>   The woman now admire,
>   Clothed with that eternal Sun
>   Which sets the worlds on fire!
>   *Bright she shall for ever shine,*
> *Enjoying, like the church above,*
>   *All the light of truth divine,*
>   *And all the fire of love.*[5]

Alexander Golitzin observes of the theology of St. Symeon the New Theologian and the Eastern Church, "That light, moreover, the splendor of divinity, pervades the whole life of the Church, in particular her sacraments and worship generally, since she is the presence in this world of the world to

---

5. *Scripture Hymns* 1762, 1:298, Hymn 944:1–4; four stanzas of a six-stanza hymn based on the Song 6:10, "Who is she that looketh forth as the morning, fair as the moon, clear as the sun, and terrible as an army with banners?" Italics added for emphasis.

come."[6] Though Wesley is not speaking of the sacraments and the worship of the church in the above poem per se, his poem most certainly affirms the spirit of Golitzin's statement.

God's Illumination Transforms Within and Without

In the previous chapter we observed that Wesley perceives the indwelling nature of God to have an effect on the outward appearance. It changes human demeanor and the way one appears to others. This is a distinct result of changing human nature into divine nature.

> 12. The promise stands for ever sure,
> *And we shall in thine image shine,*
> Partakers of a nature pure,
> Holy, and perfect, and divine,
> In Spirit joined to thee the Son,
> As thou art with thy Father one.[7]

Visibility is unquestionably an important aspect of deification, not in the sense of personal pride, but rather in the sense that as one is assimilated into the nature of God one's countenance changes, and perhaps even one's body language is transformed. One radiates the divine nature of holiness, perfection, and love in all one is and does.

In a fascinating poem titled "A Dialogue of Angels and Men" Wesley addresses the illumination of human beings that transpires in the process of partaking of God's nature.

> A: As gods we did in glory shine,
> Before the world began:
> M: *Our nature too becomes divine,*
> *And God himself is man.*
>
> A: He clothed us in these robes of light,
> The shadow of his Son:
> M: *We with transcendent glory bright,*
> *Have Christ himself put on.*[8]

---

6. Golitzin, *On the Mystical Life*, 3:143.

7. *HSP* 1742, 234, stanza 12 of a thirteen-stanza hymn based on Isa 40:8, "The word of our God shall stand for ever."

8. Ibid., 172, stanzas 3 and 4 of a nine-stanza poem. Italics added for emphasis.

Illumination and Participation

As human "nature . . . becomes divine," transformation occurs. Once again the language of clothing oneself with Christ is used by Wesley—one puts on Christ. This emphasizes that one's exterior is changed. As previously discussed, for those whose natures have become divine there is an indwelling of God's nature—one is transformed within. Here Wesley stresses, however, that one is also transformed without; there is an accompanying exterior change. While, as often emphasized by Wesley, the nature of God may reside in one's heart and soul, it has an exterior visibility. "We with transcendent glory bright, / Have Christ himself put on." Norman Russell avers, "It is only by having Christ radiant within us that we can enter into the truth which even in the Gospels is veiled from ordinary eyes."[9]

In the above discussion of "The Incarnation and Participation in the Divine Nature," the following lines from *Nativity Hymns* 1745 were quoted in reference to the purpose of God's revelation in Jesus Christ—namely, that we might partake of the divine nature. It is to the last line of stanza 5 of Hymn 8 of that collection that we now refer.

> Made flesh for our sake,
> That we might partake
> The nature divine,
> *And again in his image, his holiness shine.*[10]

One sees that partaking of the divine nature has a visible result. There is an inward and an outward bearing of God's image, for his indwelling conveys all of God's purity, holiness, and love, which the one moving toward deification now personifies. Human beings radiate the image of God in the quest for holiness. Darkness is transformed into light through such radiance.

This transformation of the human body to "shine as lightning" is described thus in *The Homilies of St. Macarius*:

> Just as the Lord's body was glorified, when he went up the mountain and was transfigured into the glory of God and into infinite light, so the saints' bodies also are glorified and shine as lightning . . . "The glory which thou hast given to me I have given to them" (John 17:22): just as many lamps are lit from one flame, so the bodies of the saints, being members of Christ, must needs be what

---

9. Russell, *Fellow Workers with God*, 103.

10. *Nativity Hymns* 1745, 12, Hymn 8:5, stanza 5 of an eight-stanza hymn. Italics added for emphasis.

Christ is, and nothing else . . . Our human nature is transformed into the power of God, and it is kindled into fire and light.[11]

Reflecting on Isa 61, Wesley wrote a poem in which he emphasizes the mutuality or reciprocity of divine and human natures. While previously we have noted the language "put on Christ" referring to participation in the divine nature, in this poem Jesus is the one who clothes us.

> 13. *Jesus my garments hath put on,*[12]
>   Hath clothed me with the milk-white vest,
> And sanctified through faith alone,
>   And in his glorious image drest.
>
> 14. He now mine inmost soul hath turned,
>   *And bid me in his nature shine,*
> With every perfect gift adorned,
>   And all my graces are divine.[13]

The metaphors in this part of the poem have to do with outward garments and outward appearance. Yet, it is not the individual who "puts on Christ"; rather, he clothes the individual with the glorious divine image ("in his glorious image drest"). The one so clothed is to shine in his nature. How does this transpire? One is adorned with every perfect gift. Even one's graces are deified. Therefore, who one is and what one does radiate with the image of the divine. If human graces are divine, then most certainly one's most refined movements and speech reflect the nature of God, namely, divine love.

Holistic Illumination Sealed by the Spirit

The divine illumination of which Wesley speaks many times in his poetry is an illumination of one's entire being, though not instantaneous. This is not an abstract idea of spiritual renewal. It is a total experience of body and mind.

---

11. Homily 15.38, in Pseudo-Macarius, *Fifty Spiritual Homilies*, 122–23.

12. This stanza echoes a line from the *Odes of Solomon*: "And the Lord renewed me with his garment, and possessed me by His light." Charlesworth, *Odes of Solomon*, Ode 11.11. See also http://www.earlychristianwritings.com/odes.html.

13. *HSP* 1749, 1:29; from Part II, stanzas 13–14 of an eighteen-stanza hymn titled "The Sixty-First Chap[ter] of Isaiah." Italics added for emphasis.

> Come, and my whole heart renew;
> Take me now, possess me whole,
> Form the Saviour in my soul,
> In my heart thy name reveal,
> Stamp me with thy Spirit's seal,
> Change my nature into thine,
> *In me thy whole image shine.*[14]

One's whole heart is renewed and one's entire being is possessed by God. Christ is formed in the soul and God's name, the name of Love, is revealed in the heart. One is stamped with the seal of the Spirit, namely Love. One's nature is changed into the divine nature and the whole image illuminates from one's being. Wesley understood deification to be a lifelong process, and thus the divine image should shine brighter and brighter with the growing human experience. As does St. Symeon the New Theologian, Wesley views "the Christian life as growth into God's light."[15]

St. Cyril of Alexandria said, "Do not forget the Holy Ghost at the time of your illumination; He is ready to stamp your soul with His seal."[16] In lines of Wesley quoted prior to the last paragraph the application of the Spirit's seal is connected with illumination. Following the line "Stamp me with thy Spirit's seal" he says, "Change my nature into thine, / In me thy whole image shine." Wesley's language would seem quite close to that of St. Cyril. One difference, however, would be in liturgical practice, for in the eighteenth-century Church of England the practice of the anointing with oil as an act of unction or sealing of the Spirit was not a liturgical priority, and this is not what Wesley had in mind, even though the language of his poetry and the language of the Eastern Church are quite similar. Clearly, Wesley means what the Orthodox tradition understands—the Spirit imprints the divine image in us.

"Transformed into the God I See"

One cannot underestimate the importance of the visibility of the divine image in the lives of Christians for Wesley. After reading Rev 3:12, he wrote some lines pertinent to this discussion. The biblical passage states, "Him

---

14. Ibid., 1:38, lines 98–104 of a 162-line poem titled "The Beatitudes. Matthew 5:3–12." Italics added for emphasis.
15. Golitzin, *On the Mystical Life*, 3:85.
16. PG 33:1009.

that overcometh will I make a pillar in the temple of my God, and he shall go no more out: and I will write upon him the name of my God, and the name of the city of my God, which is new Jerusalem, which cometh down out of heaven from my God: and I will write upon him my new name." Part of Wesley's response to this text is found in lines cited previously:

> 3. Write upon me the name divine,
> *And let thy Father's nature shine,*
> *His image visibly exprest,*
> His glory pouring from my breast
> O'er all my bright humanity,
> *Transformed into the God I see!*[17]

How is God seen? In the image that is visibly expressed in and through human beings. God's image is "visibly expressed" and the divine glory pours from the breast of those through whom the "Father's nature shine[s]." Their humanity is overcome with the brightness of the divine image. Thus they are "transformed into the God [they] see!" One sees evidence of the deification.

Since God's nature is love and imparts love, this means that the illumination that issues from the divine image (or nature) is love itself! Love becomes visible through deification! In *Family Hymns* 1767 Wesley writes,

> 6. O let our faith and love abound,
> O let our lives to all around
>   *With purest lustre shine,*
> *That all, but us, our works may see,*
> *And give the glory, Lord, to thee,*
>   *The heavenly light divine.*[18]

All one's works are to be seen as evidence of divine light, the source of faith and love.

Wesley provides an example of ways in which God's nature is made visible through us.

> Flesh out of his flesh we are,
>   And bone out of his bone,
> Who the heavenly nature share
>   Of God's most holy Son;

---

17. *Scripture Hymns* 1762, 2:421, Hymn 842:3, stanza 3 of a five-stanza hymn.

18. *Family Hymns* 1767, 38, Hymn 38:6, titled "For a Family of Believers"; stanza 6 of a six-stanza hymn. Italics added for emphasis.

Illumination and Participation

> God doth now our hearts impress,
> Made soft, yet firm, like his above,
> Filled with all the tenderness,
> And all the strength of love.[19]

The intimacy and the mutuality of the divine and human natures in the shared relationship of which Wesley speaks is expressed thus: "Flesh out of his flesh we are, / And bone out of his bone," namely "Of God's most holy Son." Then he describes the internal and external effects of the mutually shared nature. Human hearts become soft but nevertheless firm. While they are tender, they possess all the strength of love. This means a changed demeanor. One may express tenderness but not at the expense of the strength of love. When Wesley says, "*all* the tenderness / And *all* the strength of love," he means that this is a total immersion in God's nature.

Illumination of the Sanctified

There are some instances in Wesley's poetry where a special radiance or illumination accompanies a faithful or sanctified believer while yet alive and at the time of death. In the poem "On the Death of Mrs Mary Horton,"[20] Wesley writes that others recognized her works of faith that were accompanied by a light that spread a shining luster.

> Her genuine faith by works was known
> Her light with spreading lustre shone
> > Impartial, unconfined,
> Her meat and drink his will to do,
> And trace his steps, and close pursue
> > The Friend of human kind.

At her death he writes that her head was decked with rays that originated from the grace that saved her and made her faithful to the end.

---

19. *Scripture Hymns* 1762, 2:314, Hymn 613, based on Eph 5:30, "We are members of his body, of his flesh, and out of his bones."

20. There are three drafts of Wesley's poem "On the Death of Mrs Mary Horton," which are housed at the Methodist Archive and Research Centre at the John Rylands Library, the University of Manchester. They may also be found on the website of the Center for Studies in the Wesleyan Tradition: http://www.divinity.duke.edu/initiatives-centers/cswt/wesley-texts/manuscript-verse. See draft 2, page 5 and draft 3, page 10 for the first stanza above and draft 3, page 10 for the second stanza on the following page.

> The grace which saved our happy friend,
> Which made her faithful to the end,
> > And decked her head with rays,
> We shall for us sufficient prove,
> And strive in humble fear and love,
> > To perfect holiness.

Was Mary Horton advanced in deification—so advanced in the experience of grace that she had a vision of God's uncreated light? We cannot compare her to St. Basil the Great, but is her experience of God's grace so different? It is reported that when he was praying in his cell both he and his surroundings were accompanied by an extraordinary illumination, the light of divine grace. It accompanies St. Basil at prayer and Mary Horton in works of faith.

The destiny of those who travel the path of deification, the resurrected life in Christ, is one of transfigured light:

> With him [Jesus] we walk in white,
> > We in his image shine,
> Our robes are robes of light,
> > Our righteousness divine.[21]

Light Divine

Unquestionably related to the theme of deification and illumination is Wesley's use of the metaphor "light divine." He views this light as permeating all creation: "earth beneath, and heav'n above." It is the source of God's unexhausted love and it harbors all of the divine glories.

> 1. *Eternal beam of light divine,*
> > *Fountain of unexhausted love,*
> *In whom the Father's glories shine,*
> > *Thro' earth beneath, and heav'n above!*[22]

---

21. *Redemption Hymns* 1747, 22, Hymn 16:7, lines 1–4 of stanza 7 of a seven-stanza hymn. These lines are reminiscent of Rev 3:4–5, "Thou hast a few names even in Sardis which have not defiled their garments; and they shall walk with me in white; for they are worthy. He that overcometh, the same shall be clothed in white raiment; and I will not blot out his name out of the book of life, but I will confess his name before my Father, and before his angels."

22. *HSP* 1739, 144, stanza 1 of a six-stanza hymn titled "In Affliction." Italics added for emphasis.

Illumination and Participation

"Light divine" also has the distinctive power to overcome darkness and illuminate the world. In responding to the familiar words of Matt 5:14, "You are the light of the world," Wesley's use of this metaphor most certainly has a christological meaning.

> Darkness in ourselves, we shine
>   With lustre not our own,
> *Cheer the world with light divine*
>   Reflected from that Sun,
> 'Till that Sun of righteousness
>   All his heavenly rays display,
> Universal nature bless
>   With everlasting day.[23]

Wesley emphasizes that human consciousness plays a distinctive role in the effective penetration of the human soul with light divine. While such light is the result of grace, its effective indwelling is intimately bound with the conscious fixing of one's sight on God.

> O for that single eye
>   Forever fixt on thee!
> Jesus, my want supply
>   Of true simplicity,
> *And then throughout my nature shine,*
> *And fill my soul with light divine.*[24]

These lines are Wesley's response to Matt 6:22, "If thine eye be single, thy whole body shall be full of light." This is his prayer for keenly focused vision on Jesus that seeks true simplicity, namely, the permeation of one's nature/soul with divine light.

There is "A Morning Hymn" published in *HSP* 1739, which in its opening stanza brings together numerous metaphors and expressions of divine light that culminate in Wesley's eloquent description of who the Christian is—a "transcript of the deity": Day-spring, Morning-star, Radiance, glorious dress, Light Divine, Eternal Beam. God it is who sends the light that can quell darkness, can awaken to righteousness, effect illumination by being clothed with Christ, who personifies the Radiance of Light Divine. If one

---

23. *Scripture Hymns* 1762, 2:132, Hymn 31, based on Matt 5:14. Italics added for emphasis.

24. Ibid., 2:144, Hymn 72, based on Matt 6:22.

has Christ within, one has the light divine and is thus a "transcript of the deity."

> 1. "See the Day-spring from afar
> Ushered by the Morning-star!"
> Haste; to him who sends the light,
> Hallow the remains of night.
> Souls, put on your glorious dress,
> Waking into righteousness:
> Clothed with Christ aspire to shine,
> *Radiance he of Light Divine;*
> *Beam of the Eternal Beam,*
> *He in God, and God in him!*
> *Strive we him in us to see,*
> *Transcript of the deity.*[25]

---

25. *HSP* 1739, 178; stanza 1 of a three-stanza poem titled "A Morning Hymn." Italics added for emphasis.

10

Transfiguration and Participation in the Divine Nature

Transfiguration does not play as significant a role in Charles Wesley's understanding of deification as it does for many of the church fathers. In a series of his poems on the transfiguration passages in Matthew, Mark, and Luke, however, one discovers some similarities that are worthy of discussion.

A Manifestation of God

Unquestionably for Wesley the transfiguration of Christ on Mount Tabor is a manifestation of God. Responding to Matt 17:3, "And, behold, there appeared unto them Moses and Elias talking with him," Wesley wrote,

> Moses and the prophets speak
>   And witness to our Lord,
> Him and only him we seek
>   Throughout the sacred word:
> When we find the Saviour there,
> The figures and predictions shine,
>   Seen with Christ, they all declare
>   *The Majesty Divine.*[1]

---

1. MSMT, 200–201; published posthumously in *PW*, 10:305. Italics added for emphasis.

Christ is the manifestation of "the Majesty Divine." Even more articulate is a quatrain based on Mark 9:8, "And suddenly, when they had looked round about, they saw no man any more, save Jesus only with themselves."

> Contemplating their Lord alone
> All things the saints possess in one,
> Enjoy the blissful plenitude
> *Of God in Christ, and Christ in God.*[2]

Here Wesley affirms the experience of God in prayer, a dimension of the transfiguration often underscored by the church fathers. Contemplation in prayer leads to the acknowledgment that the transfiguration is indeed a manifestation "of God in Christ, and Christ in God."

Participation through Divine Light

Wesley also addresses the divine light through which Christ's followers participate in divinity. Once again he responds to an important biblical passage of the transfiguration, Mark 9:2, "And after six days Jesus taketh with him Peter, and James, and John, and leadeth them up into an high mountain apart by themselves: and he was transfigured before them."

> 1. When six great days of God are past
>   (Which man computes six thousand years)
> Th' eternal rest begins at last,
>   And Christ with all his saints appears!
> *The members in pure light arrayed*
>   On that celestial mountain meet,
> And fashioned like their dazzling head
>   Make the triumphant church complete.
>
> 2. Thou city of the living God
>   Mother and church of the first-born,
>   Jerusalem the saints' abode,
>   To thee we languish to return,

---

2. MSMK, 97, lines 5–8 of an eight-line poem published posthumously in *PW*, 11:23. Italics added for emphasis.

> To put our glorious Saviour on,
>> *Illustrious with his lustre shine,*
>> Clear as the everlasting Sun,
>> And pure as purity divine.³

Those with Christ are arrayed in pure light and fashioned like Christ, "their dazzling head." This is a part of the journey of deification, for this experience makes "the triumphant church complete." Deification moves toward ecclesial fulfillment and completion. The new Jerusalem is "the saints' abode" and there they will shine with the Savior's luster: "Clear as the everlasting Sun, / And pure as purity divine."

Wesley's words recall a passage from *The Homilies of St. Macarius* that addresses the transfiguration of the bodies of the saints: "the saints' bodies also are glorified and shine as lightning . . . human nature is transformed into the power of God, and it is kindled into fire and light."⁴

Furthermore, Wesley affirms that transfiguration with Christ is not merely a future possibility; rather, it is a present reality.

> Who Moses and the prophets hear,
>> And Christ the sum of all receive,
>> *Transfigured shall with Christ appear,*
>> *With him in light and glory live.*
> Obtain a never-fading crown,
>> Enraptured on their Saviour gaze,
> Forever by his side sit down,
>> And talk with Jesus face to face.⁵

Those who hear Moses and the prophets and receive Christ, "the sum of all," will be transfigured with Christ and live with him in light (φῶς) and glory (δόξα). Wesley understands that the transfiguration of anyone involves faith. It is not enough to hear Moses and the prophets; one must receive Christ, who is the alpha and omega, the beginning and the end, "the sum of all."

---

3. MSMK, 94-95, published posthumously in *PW*, 11:20-21. Italics added for emphasis.

4. Homily 15.38, in Pseudo-Macarius, *Fifty Spiritual Homilies*, 122-23. See the previous chapter for a fuller translation of this passage.

5. MSMK, 95, based on Mark 9:4, "There appeared unto them Elias with Moses: and they were talking with Jesus"; published posthumously in *PW*, 11:21. Italics added for emphasis.

Transfiguration: Changed Viewer or Changed Reality?

One of the questions raised by the church fathers was whether the vision of the transfiguration implies "a change in the viewer rather than in the reality that was being viewed. The vision of the transfigured Christ, in St. Maximus' understanding, implies an internal change in those who seek spiritual knowledge."[6]

A similar understanding is found in Charles Wesley's response to Luke 9:35, "And there came a voice out of the cloud, saying, This is my beloved Son: hear him."

> 1. Him, only him, we long to hear,
>   Creator of the listening ear,
>   Who comes in Moses' place,
>   Spirit and life and power imparts,
>   And speaks into our faithful hearts
>   The words of truth and grace.
>
> 2. He doth to us his mind declare,
>   By every gospel messenger
>   His will to sinners show;
>   To heathens poor he speaks his praise,
>   He speaks by all his mysteries,
>   His life and death below.
>
> 3. He speaks by benefits bestowed;
>   We hear the language of his rod,
>   Who kindly doth reprove:
>   In trouble's storm he chides our fear,
>   And gives our fluttered hearts to hear
>   The whispering voice of love.

---

6. Russell, *Fellow Workers with God*, 102.

4. His Spirit's small and quiet voice
   Makes all our broken bones rejoice,
      Our souls to health restores;
   And then the saint renewed by grace
   Abhors himself, and hides his face,
      And silently adores.[7]

Wesley describes the internal change in those who wish to listen to the "Creator of the listening ear." It is the "beloved Son" of the Luke passage who imparts "Spirit and life and power" and communicates "the words of truth and grace" to faithful hearts. One is internally and intellectually transformed, for the Son declares his mind and will to sinners. This communication transpires through all the divine mysteries—the mysteries of his life and death on earth.

The internal change is quite dramatic, for the "whispering voice of love" one hears in the beloved Son's speech rebukes fears in times of trouble and calms anxious hearts. Furthermore, his Spirit restores "our souls to health," and when one has been renewed by grace, one receives the gift of humility and "silently adores."

Remembering Peter's words (Mark 9:5), "Master, it is good for us to be here," Wesley stresses the internal dimension of revelation with the couplet "When Christ doth to the soul appear, / How good, how pleasant to be here!"

A Foretaste of the World to Come

Wesley poetically crafts a vision of God through the transfiguration experience that is a foretaste of the world to come. There are many spiritual testimonies, particularly among the monastic fathers, to the efficacy of the vision of divine light. Wesley's vision of God envisages the transfigured life "surrounded with the golden blaze, / Hid in the secret of his face." It is an awe-inspiring vision, as Wesley's reflections on Mark 9:6, "For he wist not what to say; for they were sore afraid," reveal.

---

7. MSLK, 134–35; published posthumously in *PW*, 11:185–86.

> What endless scenes of wonder rise
> And strike with rapturous surprise,
> When Jesus face to face we see
> In all his pomp and majesty!
> Angels adore the King of kings
> Their faces shadowing with their wings,
> And saints th' o'erpowering vision prove,
> In deepest awe of speechless love![8]

The transfiguration experience is visual and auditory. Mark 9:7 stresses the latter: "And there was a cloud that overshadowed them: and a voice came out of the cloud, saying, This is my beloved Son: hear him." Wesley stresses both dimensions of the vision.

> 1. Surrounded with the golden blaze,
>   Hid in the secret of his face,
>   Received with the lucid cloud,
>   Caught to the bosom of our God,
>   A voice shall bless us from the throne,
>   "This is my well-beloved Son,
>   Th' essential Truth and Life Divine,
>   Through everlasting ages thine."
>
> 2. Faithful and good, thy Saviour hear,
>   And seeing live, all eye, all ear.
>   Hear him, and let thy joys abound,
>   And fall transported at the sound,
>   The utmost powers of music prove,
>   Be fed, be feasted with his love;
>   And while eternity glides on
>   Thy banquet is but just begun.[9]

In the transfiguration one encounters "essential Truth and Life Divine." The latter words ("Life Divine") are precisely those Wesley uses in his definition of religion, "participation in/of the life divine," his equivalent for deification. Thus, at the transfiguration "Life Divine" is revealed to those

---

8. MSMK, 96; published posthumously in *PW*, 11:22.
9. MSMK, 97; published posthumously in *PW*, 11:22.

Transfiguration and Participation

who are surrounded by the golden blaze, the light of God's countenance. Thus to be transfigured with Christ is an integral part of the journey of deification.

Transfiguration: Sharing Christ's Passion and Suffering

To share in the glory of Christ means that we must also share in his passion and suffering. The thought of the cross tempers the delight of the transfiguration's ecstatic joy.

> 1. In momentary majesty
> My Saviour on the mount I see,
> As on his dazzling throne,
> But when the glorious God appears,
> He still remains the man of tears,
> And speaks of death alone.
>
> 2. May this alone my thoughts employ
> In triumph of ecstatic joy,
> And temper the delight;
> The moment that transports me hence,
> And bids eternity commence,
> Be ever in my sight.[10]

Furthermore, any true vision of the kingdom of God cannot bypass Christ's suffering, for we too bear his cross.

> The image of the earthy now
> The death we in our bodies bear,
> And daily on his cross we bow,
> The kingdom of our Lord to share;
> The image of the heavenly Man,
> Our bodies, spiritual as his
> In that sabbatic day shall gain
> With fullness of immortal bliss.[11]

---

10. MSLK, 132, based on Luke 9:31, "Who appeared in glory, and spake of his decease which he should accomplish at Jerusalem"; published posthumously in *PW*, 11:183.

11. MSMK, 95, based on Mark 9:3, "And his raiment became shining, exceeding white as snow; so as no fuller on earth can white them"; published posthumously in *PW*, 11:21.

"The radiant humanity of the Lord shows the apostles the destiny that awaits them. The Lord can now go to his suffering and death and the apostles can follow him, confident in the glory that can only be attained through sharing the Cross."[12]

Daniel A. Keating appropriately emphasizes the centrality of the cross in one's growth in deification. "Deification is not a bypassing of the Cross or a passage to glory that avoids sharing in Christ's suffering and death. Because deification means being progressively conformed to the image of Christ, there is no route to this transformation apart from participation in the suffering, death, and resurrection of Christ."[13]

The anticipation of the transfiguration as the fulfillment of the present and the age to come is eloquently summarized in Wesley's prayer based on Luke 9:28, "And it came to pass about an eight days after these sayings, he took Peter and John and James, and went up into a mountain to pray."

1. Thy kingdom, Lord, I fain would see:
    O carry up my soul with thee,
        Above my body raise,
    From earth's tumultuous scenes remove,
    Bear to the holy mountain above,
        And then unveil my face.

2. Thou only by thy prayer and blood
    Canst bring me to the smiling God,
        Reveal my sins forgiven,
    And bless me with that rapturous sight
    Which makes the saints' supreme delight,
        Which makes a heaven of heaven.[14]

While this chapter has shown similarities between Wesley's theology of the transfiguration and the church fathers, his thought is by no means as organized and developed as St. Gregory Palamas' teaching of Taboric light whereby "purified Christians, due to the uncreated energies of God, are able to be transformed into a sharing of the light that Jesus radiated on Mount Tabor through the process of divinization as they yield to the

---

12. Russell, *Fellow Workers with God*, 111.
13. Keating, *Deification and Grace*, 87.
14. MSLK, 131; published posthumously in *PW*, 11:183.

divine indwelling presence of the Trinity."[15] Nevertheless, Wesley clearly understands that Christ's committed followers share in the light radiated by Jesus, which is part of the process of deification affirmed and enabled by the indwelling Trinity.

---

15. Maloney, *Gold, Frankincense, and Myrrh*, 174.

11

Sanctification and Participation in the Divine Nature

When one comes to the subject of sanctification in Charles Wesley's works, is it to be understood as an integral part of participation in the divine nature, as is generally the case in the Eastern Church, or is sanctification to be understood separately or perhaps as a parallel path?

Sanctification: Instantaneous or Gradual?

First it must be said that sanctification for Charles Wesley is the Christian's lifelong pilgrimage—hence, it is a goal toward which one gradually moves throughout one's life. It is here that Charles stood at odds with his brother John, who desired to leave open the possibility of instantaneous or sudden sanctification. Charles expended an extensive literary effort to defend his position on gradual sanctification when he published the two-volume work *Scripture Hymns* 1762. Throughout their publishing careers John was usually the final editor of his brother's poetry; however, in the case of the 1762 volumes Charles refused to let John edit them before publication. He knew that in these poems he was often addressing "perfection" and "sanctification," on which he and John had significant differences of opinion, for Charles saw no option whatsoever for instantaneous sanctification or perfection. Quite understandably, if he viewed participation in the divine nature as a gradual process, sanctification would necessarily be so understood as well.

One example suffices to illustrate the significant difference between the brothers. As a response to Prov 4:18, "The path of the just is as the shining light, that shineth more and more unto the perfect day," Charles wrote,

Sanctification and Participation

> Shall we mistake the morning-ray
> Of grace for the full blaze of day?
> Or humbly walk in Jesu's sight,
> Glad to receive the *gradual* light,
> More of his grace and more to know,
> In faith and in experience grow,
> 'Till all the life of Christ we prove,
> And *lose ourselves* in perfect love!¹

John Wesley made numerous editorial notes in the margins of his own copy of the 1762 volumes, which is located among the small library holdings in his house in London. No doubt many of these were changes John would have made to Charles's texts, had he been allowed to do so. There is a significant marginal note in John's copy for the fourth line of the above poem: "Glad to receive the *gradual* light." He wrote the word *sudden* to go after *gradual*. No doubt both brothers shared the view that the path to holiness or sanctification involved lifelong growth in knowledge, faith, and experience. Nevertheless, John wished to leave open the possibility of "sudden" light as well as "gradual light." For Charles this was not an option. Along the path to holiness one received "gradual light." Hoping to correct the erroneous view of instantaneous sanctification, he undertook the lengthy two-volume work *Scripture Hymns* 1762, with 2,349 poems based on passages from all books of the Bible.

Charles's preface to the two volumes makes clear his intention.

> Several hymns are intended to prove, and several to guard, the doctrine of Christian Perfection. I durst not publish one without the other.
>
> In the latter sort I use some severity, not against particular persons, but against enthusiasts and antinomians, who by not living up to their profession, "give" abundant "occasion to them that seek it" [2 Cor 11:12], and "cause the truth to be evil spoken of" [2 Pet 2:2].
>
> Such there have been, in every age, in every revival of religion. But this does in no wise justify the men who put darkness for light, and light for darkness; who call the wisdom of God foolishness, and all real religion Enthusiasm.
>
> "When the wheat springs up, the tares also appear, and both grow together until the harvest" [Matt 13:26f.]: yet is there an

---

1. *Scripture Hymns* 1762, 1:284, Hymn 901. Italics added for emphasis.

> essential difference between them. This occasions a difference in my expressions; and as great a seeming contradiction, as when I declare with St. Paul, "A man is justified by faith, and not by works" [Gal 2:16]; and with St. James, "A man is justified by works, and not by faith only" [Jas 2:24].
>
> My desire is, "rightly to divide the word of Truth" [2 Tim 2:15]: but who is sufficient for these things?" [2 Cor 2:16] Who can check the self-confident, without discouraging the self-dissident? I trust in God, that none of the latter will take to themselves what belongs to the former only.
>
> READER, if God ministers grace to thy soul thro' any of these hymns, give Him glory, and offer up a prayer for the weak instrument, that whenever I finish my course, I may depart in peace, having seen in JESUS CHRIST his great Salvation.[2]

It is important to emphasize, however, that Charles's interest in correcting misdirected ideas about perfection was not primarily directed toward his brother John. A vibrant perfection controversy[3] arose circa 1760 whereby some of the Methodist constituents were claiming to be fully perfected. Thomas Maxfield and George Bell claimed "that the perfected Christian was without sin and, once perfected, would persist in this angelic state. Their view led to a dangerous combination of assertive infallibility and blatant antinomianism."[4] Such misguided ideas were much more serious than Charles's disagreement with John on instantaneous sanctification. Written at the height of such controversy Charles's preface to the 1762 volumes makes his very explicit responses understandable. He speaks as only a gentleman would: "I use some severity, not against particular persons, but against Enthusiasts and Antinomians, who by not living up to their profession, *give* abundant *occasion to them that seek it, and cause the truth to be evil spoken of.*"

Charles's response to Mark 4:28, "The earth bringeth forth fruit of herself; first the blade, then the ear, after that the full corn in the ear," underscores his opposition to the possibility of instantaneous sanctification.

> Thou dost not say, the seed springs up
> Into an instantaneous crop;
> But waiting long for its return,
> We see the blade, the ear, the corn;

---

2. Preface to *Scripture Hymns* 1762. The pages of the Preface are not numbered.
3. See Heitzenrater, *Wesley and the People Called Methodists*, 209–11.
4. Ibid., 209.

Sanctification and Participation

The weak; and *then* the stronger grace,
And *after* that full holiness.⁵

Though there are many such references in *Scripture Hymns* 1762, one additional example is sufficient to discern Charles Wesley's posture in this matter. Once again he responds to Scripture, namely Jas 5:7, "Behold, the husbandman waiteth for the precious fruit of the earth, and hath long patience for it, until he receive the early and latter rain." He uses an agrarian metaphor to stress that one who tills the earth cannot expect the best fruit until the latter rain comes. The tiller must patiently wait.

"But may we not at once spring up,
"In sudden holiness mature?"
Nay; but we must the flattering hope
Renounce, and to the end endure:
The ripest fruit cannot appear,
Until the latter rain come down,
And faith's almighty Finisher
Our patience with perfection crown.⁶

Even so, it would be incorrect to assume that Charles does not anticipate sanctification in this life. He holds in tension realizable and unrealizable holiness. He writes, "This hope of holiness, / Still may I hold it fast."⁷ He knows it is within God's power to fulfill the promise of Scripture: "You shall therefore be holy, for I am holy" (Lev 11:45).

Faithful, I account thee, Lord,
To thy sanctifying word,
I shall soon be as thou art,
Holy both in life and heart,
Perfect holiness attain,
All thine image *here* regain,
Love my God entirely *here*,
Blameless then in heaven appear.⁸

---

5. *Scripture Hymns* 1762, 2:201, Hymn 286. The italicized words in lines 5 and 6 are italicized in the first edition.

6. Ibid., 2:388, Hymn 758:2, stanza 2 of a two-stanza hymn.

7. Ibid., 2:318, Hymn 622.

8. Ibid., 2:326, Hymn 638, based on 1 Thess 5:24, "Faithful is he that calleth you, who also will do it." The italicized word *here* appears in the first edition.

Sanctification and Deification: Equivalents?

It has been observed by some scholars that the Wesleyan concept of sanctification is similar to the Orthodox concept of deification.[9] Tore Meistad describes the similarities as follows:

> The Wesleyan concepts of holiness and sanctification clearly resemble the Eastern Orthodox concept of *theosis* rather than the Western tendency to understand sanctification as a perfect fulfillment of God's will as prescribed in the law. In the Wesleyan understanding, God's sanctifying grace works an actual transformation of the human person as s/he is penetrated by fresh, divine life. The metaphors of living by the power of Christ's resurrection (Philippians 3:10), experiencing the restoration of heaven and earth, and the perfect renewal of love, all express the experience of this transformation due to God's re-creation of the sinner. The Wesleyan notion of Christian perfection resembles almost word for word St Symeon the New Theologian's elaboration of *theosis*. Rather than speaking of the believer's union with God, Charles Wesley's focus is on the believer's mystical experience of being in communion with God.[10]

There can be no question that the similarities of the two traditions are indeed real, and in Charles's case this is most certainly so. Meistad is incorrect, however, to aver that Charles Wesley does not speak "of the believer's union with God." Indeed, he often does so. Unfortunately, in most discussions of sanctification in the Wesleyan tradition, the plethora of references to participation in the divine nature and union with God in Charles Wesley's literature already mentioned in this study are often not examined carefully, especially in relation to the doctrine of participation in the divine nature.

There is one poem in which Charles links holiness and deification, and it provides an important emphasis of Charles's theology that is very close to Orthodox theology.

> He wills, that I should holy be:
> *That holiness I long to feel,*
> That *full divine conformity*
> To all my Saviour's righteous will:

---

9. See Maddox, *Responsible Grace*, 122, 176–90; Ashanin, *Essays on Orthodox Christianity*, 90.

10. Meistad, "Missiology of Charles Wesley," 211.

Sanctification and Participation

> See, Lord, the travail of thy soul
> > Accomplished in the change of mine,
> And plunge me, every whit made whole,
> > In all the depths of love divine.[11]

Here holiness is equivalent to full divine conformity to Christ's will. According to 1 Thess 4:3 ("This is the will of God, even your sanctification") on which the poem is based, the divine will is sanctification. Are then participation (in the divine nature) and sanctification to be understood as synonyms in the writings of Charles Wesley? How close is his thought to that of the Eastern Church? John A. McGuckin maintains that

> In the Greek Christian understanding, the concept of deification is the process of sanctification of Christians whereby they become progressively conformed to God; a conformation that is ultimately demonstrated in the glorious transfiguration of the "just" in the heavenly kingdom, when immortality and a more perfect vision (and knowledge and experience) of God are clearly manifested in the glorification (δόξα) of the faithful.[12]

Can we say that in the theology of Charles Wesley "the concept of deification is the process of sanctification of Christians whereby they become progressively conformed to God"? If we cannot say this unequivocally about Charles Wesley's theology, we can indeed affirm it.

---

11. *Scripture Hymns* 1762, 2:324, Hymn 631. Italics added for emphasis.
12. McGuckin, "Strategic Adaptation of Deification," 95.

12

Participation in the Divine Nature as Progression

Progression toward Participation

Praxis in Orthodoxy is the first stage of *theosis* and consists essentially in practical guidance one receives at the outset of the journey toward deification. It may include prayer, searching the Scriptures, receiving Holy Communion, fasting, and fellowship in community. Quite similar to Orthodox *praxis* is the Wesleyan view of acts of piety, that is, spiritual disciplines that guide one toward holiness and perfection. In the Wesleyan tradition the acts of piety are not limited to the outset of the journey toward participation in the divine nature but provide lifelong practical guidance on the path toward sanctification, which, as already noted, in Charles Wesley's theology is a part of the journey of participation. They are the spiritual disciplines whereby one's inner being is cleansed of all worldly passions and distractions so that God's love can be nurtured to its fullest potential through the power of the indwelling Holy Spirit.

Charles Wesley is keenly aware of the need to subdue unruly passions, stubborn wills, and the carnal mind so that love may command our hearts.

> 1. Giver of concord, Prince of Peace,
>   Meek, lamb-like Son of God,
>   Bid our unruly passions cease,
>   O quench them with thy blood.
>
> 2. Rebuke the seas, the tempest chide,
>   Our stubborn wills control,
>   Beat down our wrath, root out our pride,
>   And calm our troubled soul.

Participation as Progression

3. Subdue in us the carnal mind,
    Its enmity destroy,
With cords of love th' old Adam bind,
    And melt him into joy.

4. Us into closest union draw,
    And in our inward parts
Let kindness sweetly write her law,
    Let love command our hearts.

5. O let thy love our hearts constrain!
    Jesus the crucified,
What hast thou done our hearts to gain,
    Languished, and groaned, and died!

6. Who would not now pursue the way
    Where Jesu's footsteps shine?
Who would not own the pleasing sway
    Of charity divine?

7. Saviour, look down with pitying eyes,
    Our jarring wills control;
Let cordial, kind affections rise,
    And harmonize the soul.

8. Thee let us feel benignly near,
    With all thy quick'ning powers,
The sounding of thy bowels hear,
    And answer thee with ours.

9. O let us find the ancient way
    Our wond'ring foes to move,
And force the heathen world to say,
    "See how these Christians love."[1]

---

1. *HSP* 1740, 118–19. The poem is based on 1 John 3:18, "Little children, love one another."

Subduing these forces that easily distract one's inner self from being fully consumed by God's love transpires by God's grace and is a lifelong struggle. Hence, the path toward participation in the divine nature is long and tedious, but rewarded by the recognition of opposing forces: "See how these Christians love." This is the fruit of participation.

This prayer reveals Wesley's confidence that through contemplative prayer we may be so constrained by the love of God in our hearts that we overcome misguided passions, we transcend the corporeal state, and we participate in the divine nature. Thus we are drawn into closest union with God (stanza 4) "in our inward parts," and the love of Christ commands our hearts and controls our jarring wills. What Paul M. Collins says of John Wesley may also be said of Charles: "In common with Orthodox spiritual writers, Wesley [John] emphasized prayer as a means of achieving contemplation of God and the ascetic life as a means of struggling for victory over the ungodly influences of life."[2]

The Parable of the Sower in Mark 4 provides for Charles Wesley a paradigm of growth in deification. "So is the kingdom of God, as if a man should cast seed into the ground; and should sleep, and rise night and day, and the seed should spring up and grow up, he knoweth not how" (Mark 4:26–27). These words from Mark's Gospel precipitate the following lines from Wesley:

> Ye bold t' explain, describe, define
> *The progress of the life divine,*
> Your learned ignorance allow,
> And own it grows ye know not how!
> No mortal eye the manner sees
> The imperceptible degrees,
> By which our Lord conducts his plan,
> And brings us to a perfect man.[3]

It is impossible to describe and define "the progress of the life divine," or the journey toward participation in the divine nature. How life divine progresses is a mystery. It emerges indistinguishably, and, as intelligent as one may be, it is impossible to discern how this transpires. It is impossible to see the progression with one's own eyes. Its varying degrees are not perceptible, for it is God who directs the path and brings us to perfection. As Dumitru

---

2. Collins, *Partaking in Divine Nature*, 153.
3. *Scripture Hymns* 1762, 2:200-201, Hymn 285. Italics added for emphasis.

Stăniloae avers, "Deification never stops, but continues beyond the ultimate limits of the power of human nature, to the infinite."[4] Chris Jensen describes the process more fully as follows: "Deification, then, is the summit of a gradual process by which human beings are reintegrated into the life of God, beginning with the restoration of God's image through baptism and continuing with purification of heart and illumination by divine grace."[5]

Hallmarks of Participation of the Divine Nature

What this study has shown thus far underscores the progression of growing in and partaking of the life divine.

1. Charles Wesley has defined religion as "participation of the divine nature." Furthermore, "in all our thoughts, and words, and works" we are "to be partakers of the divine nature." This presupposes that God dwells within us through the witness of the Holy Trinity: Father, Son, and Holy Ghost. At no point, however, does Wesley affirm that partaking of the divine nature is a "once for all" experience in which the divine nature is fully imbibed by a believer. Rather, it is a progressive experience that lasts a lifetime.

2. In his *Nativity Hymns* 1745 Charles affirms that the purpose of the incarnation is participation in God's nature. "Made Flesh for our Sake, / That we might partake / The Nature Divine, / And again in his Image, his Holiness shine." The incarnation makes possible the union of human and divine natures. Wesley says, "Our nature too becomes divine, / And God himself is man." This is God's step toward deification on our behalf. The incarnation is, however, the beginning not the end of deification.

3. Through the sacraments of the church one partakes of and grows in the divine nature. In the sacrament of baptism one becomes a partaker of the divine nature and is an inheritor of "pardon, holiness, and heaven." Wesley prays constantly for the baptized: ". . . partners of thy nature make," for he knows this is the beginning of participation in

---

4. Stăniloae, *Orthodox Spirituality*, 363.
5. Jensen, "Shine as the Sun," 52.

the divine nature, but clearly it is by God's grace, yet it does require a human response.

Another dimension of growth in sacramental participation in God's nature is the ongoing sharing in Holy Communion. Through the reception of the elements of bread and wine one participates in the divine nature. For Wesley such participation "makes Divine." In the elements, he says, we taste "Life Divine." Furthermore, the Holy Spirit is "transmitted in the sacred wine." Hence, one constantly prays, "Fill us with immortal meat, / and make thy nature known." This is a perpetual prayer, for God's nature is never fully known.

4. The divine nature in which we participate is the Holy Trinity. Wesley says that the "understanding mind" seeks "to know thy nature and thy name, / One God in Persons Three." Even so it is a mystery, for we are "mystically one with thee, / Transcript of the Trinity." Holiness is enabled through the indwelling of the Holy Spirit and "Fashioned after my Creator, / God as I am known to know." Indeed, the Holy Trinity is the center of one's existence: "Draw me now into my centre; . . . / Father, Son, and Spirit enter." This is the center toward which we are continually drawn in the journey of participation.

5. Participation in God's nature does not transpire in isolation, but rather within the life of community, the church—the body of Christ. It has an ecclesial context. Hence, it is individual and corporate. Wesley writes, "Change my nature into thine, / In me thy whole image shine." Through the Eucharist, he avers, God's nature is "to thy church made known."

The unity of the body of Christ is underscored when he says, "For us he uses all his Powers, / And all He has, or is, is ours." Hence, the church prays, "Hear us, who thy nature share, / Who thy mystic body are; / Join us in one spirit, join." Since the church is not fully joined in one spirit, participation in the divine nature is not complete; hence, it is an ongoing process, a goal toward which the church is moving. Therefore, one continues to pray Wesley's prayer: "Join us in one spirit, join."

6. Since God's nature is love ("God is love," 1 John 4:8), it is love that joins the divine and human natures. Wesley affirms, "Thy nature, and

thy name is Love." It is the initiative of God's love that enables participation. Through love we come to know who God is. It enables us to become Godlike. Wesley pleads, "change me into love."

When he prays, "Thy nature, dearest Lord, impart, / Come quickly from above," this is not limited to a specific time, for it is a perpetual prayer. There is always the need for the immediate imparting of God's nature, namely, love. This is one's constant prayer on the path toward sanctification and perfection. Love destroys distinctions among humankind and enables affection for all persons. Such love is not passive but actively involves Christ's followers with one another, community, and society.

7. Participation in the divine nature changes our appearance. Transformation may be internal but it is also external. We "bear the new nature the image divine." And this image is "visibly exprest." The divine image shines inwardly and outwardly, so that others see the evidence of the transformation. Wesley says, "We with transcendent glory bright, / Have Jesus Christ put on." A major result of this is "all my graces are divine." These graces will be visible to others.

Participation in God's nature involves growth, development, and progression. If all of our graces are deified, every aspect of our demeanor and talents, this cannot be an instantaneous experience, but rather a progressive one. The visible expression of such transformation will slowly but surely be obvious to others, not because we will it, but because of the grace of God's initiative whose nature we bear.

8. Is it possible to affirm that participation in the divine nature and sanctification are one and the same in Charles Wesley's theology? Are these parallel paths or the same path for him? The discussion thus far has shown that Wesley unquestionably affirms that the Christian progressively, not instantaneously, becomes conformed to God. Thus, the pathway to sanctification is an integral aspect of participation in the divine nature, and it is by no means separate from it.

Summary

Though oversimplified, an overview of Charles Wesley's prose and poetry provides the following progressive outline of participation in the divine nature:

1. The incarnation enables participation.
2. Through baptism one becomes a partaker of God's nature.
3. Through Holy Communion one continues to partake of the divine nature.
4. Through the indwelling of the Holy Trinity one grows in knowledge and understanding of the divine nature.
5. The church is the context for growth in partaking of the divine nature.
6. Growing in the knowledge and practice of divine love, one comes to know God's nature and name: love.
7. Participation in the divine nature transforms human appearance and demeanor, so that others see that Christ's followers have "put on" Christ. Nevertheless, all of one's graces are not transformed in the blink of an eye. The deification of all our graces takes a lifetime.

Such views of a progressive deification certainly place Charles Wesley's thought in concert with the ideas of Origen, St. Ephrem the Syrian, St. Gregory of Nyssa, and other church fathers. But when it comes to what it means to share in the divine nature—namely, no longer to be governed by human passions, and to enjoy incorruptibility—does Wesley's theology continue in concert with the church fathers? Most certainly a vital goal of the sanctified life guided by the Holy Spirit, and lived as a transcript of the Trinity, is freedom from human passions and incorruptibility. Yet, one cannot claim this for oneself; it is a gift received through one's knowledge and experience of the Christ of the incarnation.

Wesley believed that it is possible for our minds to be so filled with Christ that we may rise above all material realities of this world, so that our vision of God is clearer and through this clearer vision we participate more deeply in God's nature. This requires commitment to prayer and contemplation. The deifying quality of divine love, God's nature, cannot be underestimated. Love has one of the most significant roles in the process of participation in God's nature.

Participation as Progression

All of the dimensions of the progression toward deification do not transpire instantaneously or immediately. They comprise the Christian's life journey—marked by humility, repentance, prayer, works of charity, and sharing in the sacraments—within the church by God's grace toward sanctification and participation in the divine nature.

13

Evaluating Charles Wesley's Views of Participation in the Light of the Early Church Fathers

CHARLES WESLEY'S EXTANT LITERATURE provides no direct evidence of his engagement with the divergent positions of the patristic era pertaining to the use of appropriate language for accessing the divine nature. Wesley does not use the word *deification* in his writings and does not reveal the reasons behind his preference for the phrases "participation in/of the divine nature" and "partakers of the life divine." Given his strong biblical orientation, however, his preference for the words from 2 Pet 1:4 is understandable, though the influence of Hooker, Andrewes, and Scougal undergirded such a preference.

Similarities and Differences

Wesley apparently did not see his theological task as developing technical language for these ideas, for he was expressing them primarily through poetry, much like St. Ephrem in the Syrian tradition. He does not craft a systematic exposition of the doctrine of participation, but he does emphasize many of the essential elements of the patristic understanding of deification or *theosis*. Furthermore, in the light of his poetry it would appear fair to say that participation in the divine nature is at the core of Wesley's theological vision. For him it is the goal and purpose of creation, which was a primary perspective of St. Maximus the Confessor, and others before him, though St. Maximus preferred the word *deification*.[1] Of course, a unified approach to deification in the early church did not exist. The various perspectives

---

1. See Russell, *Doctrine of Deification*, 267–68.

on *theosis*, deification, or participation in the divine nature are nuanced in many ways by the church fathers.

There is a primary difference between Charles Wesley and the church fathers on the origin of the biblical basis for deification or *theosis*. The idea or teaching on *theosis* emerged at the outset from an exegesis of Ps 81:6[2] and was only later confirmed by 2 Pet 1:4. It is interesting that in all of Charles Wesley's literature (journal, sermons, poetry), nowhere does he refer to Ps 81:6. He begins his interpretation of participation in the divine nature directly from 2 Pet 1:4.

What are the resources that influenced Wesley's choice of language for participation in the divine nature? No doubt he was strongly influenced in this regard by Richard Hooker, Lancelot Andrewes, and Henry Scougal. Most certainly he could have been introduced to many of the Greek church fathers through Hooker's *Ecclesiastical Polity*, where they are often quoted. Given Wesley's reliance on biblical interpretation as the basis of his theological perspectives, he reflects a preference for the language of 2 Pet 1:4. Like Origen, Wesley concentrated on biblical exegesis, and unlike Justin and St. Clement of Alexandria, he was less inclined to rely on philosophy. Even so, as this study has already shown, Wesley shares many theological roots with Eastern Orthodox traditions.

Theological Roots: Commonalities and Differences

One finds in Wesley's writings certain aspects of the patristic-era discussion of deification.

1. He juxtaposes such opposites as created and uncreated, mortal and immortal, human and divine.

2. He appears to have a preference for speaking of God's image rather than likeness, though there are hints of the latter here and there in his literature.

3. While offering no philosophical background for the use of the terms "divine essence" and "divine energy," one finds a limited use of these terms in Wesley's poetry. His writings do not reflect an overt awareness

---

2. Mosser, "The Earliest Patristic Interpretation of Psalm 82, Jewish Antecedent, and the Origins of Christian Deification."

of the controversy that culminated in Gregory Palamas' eloquent delineation of these terms and their subsequent influence on Orthodox theology.

4. Of the three different ways in which deification was understood during the patristic period—nominal, analogical, and metaphorical[3]—only the last of these seems to apply to Wesley. Generally speaking, he does not use the word *god* for humans as an honorific title, which eliminates the nominal and analogical approaches. However, he does seem to favor a metaphorical approach, which sees the possibility of human transformation based on participation in the divine nature. Hence, for Wesley participation reflects God's purpose for all humankind and delineates the closest possible tie between the divine and human. Unlike Clement of Alexandria, he does not affirm that when one experiences deification by way of heavenly teaching and becomes perfected after the divine likeness, one (though still in the flesh) has become a "god."[4] Wesley only refers to the possibility of becoming "god" in union with God beyond death.

5. The "exchange formula"—God becomes human in order that humans may become divine—is very much a part of Charles Wesley's theology of participation. In this regard the incarnation is the heart of the divine-human synergy. This surfaces numerous times in his poetry. He most certainly shares the view of Ephrem the Syrian: "He gave us divinity, we gave him humanity."[5]

6. The sacraments of baptism and Holy Communion express important relational aspects of deification in the Wesleyan and Orthodox traditions. Through the grace bestowed by way of these sacraments one's knowledge and experience of the divine nature are enhanced. Even so, Charles Wesley does not appear to share the view of St. Irenaeus and St. Clement of Alexandria that the baptized have been adopted by God as "gods" and as far as possible have been separated from all that is human. Wesley would generally express the adoption as "sons of God,"[6] as in Article 27 of the Articles of Religion. He does not

---

3. See Collins, *Partaking in Divine Nature*, 51.
4. Clement of Alexandria, *Stromateis*, 7.101.4. See *The Seventh Book of the Stromateis*.
5. St. Ephrem the Syrian, *Hymns on Paradise*, 72.
6. As in the language of Article 27, "Of Baptism," of the Articles of Religion of the

share the view that in baptism one has been separated from all that is human. It may be surprising, however, for some to learn that Wesley does refer to those who have partaken of the divine nature as "gods" but does so only in reference to an ultimate future union with God. In the final stanza of a six-stanza poem titled "Hymn for Christian Friends" Wesley writes,

6. Thy kingdom restore
    In the spirit of power,
That prays, and exults, and gives thanks evermore;
    Thy nature make known,
    And perfect in one,
And receive us as gods to a share of thy throne.[7]

Who are those to be received "as gods" but the baptized who have been sustained by the Eucharist in the ecclesial community! They are those to whom the divine nature has been made known and who have been perfected in one. Wesley prays that these persons will be received "as gods to a share of thy throne." This is their eschatological destiny. Here Wesley is in concert with St. Basil and Origen, whose understanding of deification as a gradual process refers to human beings as "gods" only in their ultimate state.

For Charles Wesley there is dynamic participation in the divine nature at baptism through the reception of the Holy Spirit who indwells the baptized. Thus baptism is the beginning of a lifelong continuum of the activity of divine grace in and through the Holy Trinity who enables sanctification and opens the path toward perfection. This places Wesley's understanding of baptism alongside that of St. Cyril of Alexandria, though Wesley, as just noted, does not use the word *gods* to signify the baptized immediately after baptism.

One finds numerous references among the church fathers to Holy Communion as a source of deification. While St. Maximus the Confessor, St. John of Damascus, and St. Dionysius "each in different ways understand deification in 'mystical' terms, they all emphasize the collective and ecclesial accessibility of deification for all believers in

---

Church of England: "They that receive Baptism rightly are grafted into the Church; the promises of the forgiveness of sin, and of our adoption to be the sons of God by the Holy Ghost, are visibly signed and sealed."

7. *HSP* 1749, 2:293; Hymn 25 [Hymn for Christian Friends]. Italics added for emphasis.

the sacraments of baptism and Eucharist. Intimacy with the divine is understood to be personal and corporate."[8] In Charles Wesley's view deification transpires through baptism and the Eucharist but also through private experience.

Most certainly Wesley shares with many of the church fathers a relational concept of participation in the divine nature through the sacraments of baptism and Holy Communion. While it appears from his poetry that he understood participation in mystical terms, the sacraments emphasize for him the collective and ecclesial accessibility of participation. There can be no personal relationship that is not also corporate. Participation involves an essential social element.

Hence, "deification is not something that can be attained in isolation without the social dimension. The ecclesial life is needed. Baptism deifies us in a nominal sense by endowing us with the name of Christ. Baptism also bestows the Holy Spirit. The reception of the Eucharist consolidates this process."[9]

Without question Charles Wesley's theology is sacramental, for he sees the sacraments as the seat of participation in the divine nature. Is he, however, a mystic, given his sacramental perspective, his view of the Trinity as a "mystical plurality," and his view of the church as God's "mystic body"? He speaks of the "mystic incarnation" and of the "mystic power of godliness," and he describes union with God as "mystically one with thee, / Transcript of the Trinity." Though it would be going too far to label him a mystic, most certainly he espouses a mystical theology.[10] His brother John may have feared that he was leaning too much toward mysticism, as editorial omission by John of the following portion of a stanza of one of Charles's hymns in the 1780 *Collection* noted earlier might suggest:

> *Mystically one with thee,*
> *Transcript of the Trinity,*
> Thee let all our nature own
> One in Three, and Three in One.[11]

8. Collins, *Partaking in Divine Nature*, 110.

9. Russell, *Doctrine of Deification*, 294–95.

10. Gordon Wakefield maintains, "With the Orthodox parallel in mind we ought perhaps to speak of the 'mystical theology' of Charles Wesley, that is, a theology which derives from more than intellectual processes, but from the heart, which transcends reason" ("Charles Wesley's Spirituality," 86).

11. *HSP* 1740, 188, Part 1:1, the last four lines of stanza 1.

Evaluating Charles Wesley's Views

Charles Wesley's theology, like that of St. Basil, "is not an abstract reflection, but a concrete way of living the mystery in the deepening of the faith through prayer and the renunciation of one's own will. It is a way of the submission of the human to the divine will, which allows the grace of the Holy Spirit to impregnate human nature."[12]

7. Deification is the *raison d'être* of the incarnation. Though Wesley prefers "participation in the divine nature" to "deification," his views regarding the synergy of the incarnation are largely in concert with St. Basil, St. Gregory of Nazianzus, and St. Gregory of Nyssa. Wesley's perspectives are perhaps closer to Gregory of Nyssa, who preferred *participation* to *deification* to express the emerging intimate relationship of human and divine natures. Gregory is careful to exclude "divine essence" from this relationship, stressing a union only with the divine energies. Though Wesley only addresses these categories peripherally, his persistent emphasis on the incomprehensibility of God parallels St. Gregory of Nyssa's exclusion of the divine essence from participation in the divine nature. Though Wesley does not share St. Gregory of Nazianzus' preference for the word *deification*, he does share Gregory's view that sharing in the divine nature is a gradual growth process toward fulfillment in the divine.

It is very interesting that St. Athanasius dwells on the idea of participation in the divine life, whereas St. Gregory shifts the emphasis to the imitation of Christ. In Charles Wesley's writings we find both emphases, though the former finds stronger expression in his poetry. One becomes like Christ through the sacraments.

There are also some congruences between Charles Wesley and St. Maximus the Confessor as regards the incarnation. "Using the Incarnation as his paradigm Maximos argues that the divine and human interpenetrate each other in the believer, without becoming confused, changed, divided, or separated . . . So it is axiomatic for Maximos that God became human that human beings might become god; in other words the divine kenōsis produces human theōsis."[13] Maximus says, "For just as having loosed the laws of nature supernaturally he was made low for us without change—so also shall we consequently come

---

12. N. Lossky, *Lancelot Andrewes*, quoted in Allchin, *Participation in God*, 22.
13. Collins, *Partaking in Divine Nature*, 106–7.

to be above because of him—gods as he is by the mystery of grace—altering nothing at all of our nature."[14]

While Wesley's poetry reflects his sharing of these perspectives, especially as regards *kenosis* and *theosis*, he prefers to speak of "partakers of the divine nature," rather than using the word *god* to refer to those who share in this experience, except at the time of ultimate union with God at death.

Many of Charles Wesley's perspectives regarding participation in the divine nature appear to be influenced by Richard Hooker's discussions in his *Ecclesiastic Polity*, of which Wesley owned a copy. Hooker clearly followed the tradition of the Greek Fathers, whom he often quotes, when he maintained that in the incarnation there is no blending of the human and divine natures. Though united through the sacraments, each retains its integrity. Wesley's literature reveals his preference for this view.

8. Participation in the divine nature is understood in relation to the Holy Trinity. Once again Wesley's views are in harmony with St. Maximus the Confessor, for he understands *imago dei* as *imago trinitatis*.

The Role of Intellect and Participation in the Divine Nature

In spite of the provocative theological positions on deification and participation endorsed by Richard Hooker, Lancelot Andrewes, Henry Scougal, John Wesley, Charles Wesley, and others, "the metaphor of deification did not become a common topic in the discourse and preaching in the Church of England."[15]

In his chapter "The 'Architecture' of the Metaphor in the West," Collins includes a description of the perspectives of Bernard of Clairvaux (1090–1153), which could also appropriately describe those of Charles Wesley.

> Bernard understands that mystical union does not abolish the difference between the divine and the human; rather he sees union as a union of love and of wills. Union with God is not a union of essence(s) but it is a "spiritual" union. Bernard writes with a strong emphasis on love. For Bernard the "knowledge" of God is

---

14. *Ambigua* 7, quoted in Cooper, *Body in St. Maximus the Confessor*, 112.
15. Collins, *Partaking of the Divine Nature*, 152.

Evaluating Charles Wesley's Views

connected with this love. It is an experiential rather than a theoretical knowledge of God, and it is a knowledge of God's goodness. He argues that it is not possible to know the divine essence and that this would be useless anyway. Nonetheless, union with God is a union with the Holy Trinity, and significantly he argues that the Church is the indispensable context for union. Mystical union is based upon the ongoing process of sanctification, which he understands is a lifelong growing in the love of God and neighbour. Union with God would only be consummated in the final resurrection. Bernard represents a strand in the Western tradition's diverse understanding of deification, which is rooted in an appeal to the emotions and to the experience of prayer and contemplation, as well as to the collective reality of the Church.[16]

Does Charles Wesley use the language and imagery of the patristic accounts of deification/participation? This study has shown that in many areas he does. Is deification/participation rooted in philosophy or theology? For Wesley most assuredly its roots are in Scripture and theology. What about intellectual ascent to God? Does it stand on its own or is it based on the incarnation or Christology? What are the roles of intellect and divine revelation? Without question there is a strong influence of Platonism[17] on some of the church fathers, who see salvation as being based on wisdom. For them the mind becomes the seat of the image of God. For Charles Wesley divine revelation does not nullify human intellect. The two go together. He unquestionably sees participation in the divine nature as involving human intellect, human experience, and divine revelation. His theology, however, does not reflect a strong influence of Platonism.

In a lyrical prayer published in his *Children's Hymns* 1763 and titled "At the Opening of a School in Kingswood," Charles Wesley underscores the role of intellect in the nurturing and growth of a child.

> 3. Error and ignorance remove,
>   Their blindness both of heart and mind;
>   Give them the wisdom from above,
>   Spotless, and peaceable, and kind;
>   *In knowledge pure their mind renew,*
>   *And store with thoughts divinely true.*

---

16. Ibid., 123–24.

17. Danielou, *Platonisme et théologie mystique*. See also Cherniss, *The Platonism of Gregory of Nyssa*.

4. Learning's redundant part and vain
> Be here cut off, and cast aside;
But let them, Lord, the substance gain,
> In every solid truth abide;
Swiftly acquire, and ne'er forego
The knowledge fit for man to know.

5. *Unite the pair so long disjoined,*
> *Knowledge and vital piety,*
Learning and holiness combined,
> And truth and love, let all men see,
In these, whom up to thee we give,
Thine, wholly thine, to die and live.[18]

The mind is to be a reservoir of divinely true thoughts, pure knowledge, wisdom from above, and devoid of redundant knowledge. The key to Wesley's understanding of the role of intellect in participation in the divine nature is found in stanza 5, when he says that "knowledge and vital piety" are to be united and "learning and holiness combined." The path toward holiness or sanctification for Charles Wesley, as we have already seen, is essentially equivalent to the path toward deification. Therefore, he is emphasizing the importance of intellect along this path. There is to be an intimate relationship of knowledge and everything that engages us as we participate in the divine nature: prayer, meditation, contemplation, study, participation in Holy Communion, engagement in acts of mercy.

Participation in the Divine Nature, the Goal of the Christian Faith

For Wesley the goal and purpose of the Christian faith is participation in the divine nature. The goal and purpose apply to all humankind, and participation is the means whereby humankind is redeemed. It transpires solely through God's grace but requires a human response, as the phrase "partakers of the life divine" implies.

As the exchange formula makes clear, the Son of God became the Son of Man so that we might become the sons and daughters, that is, children,

---

18. *Children's Hymns* 1763, 35–36, Hymn 40:3–5; stanzas 3–5 of a six-stanza hymn titled "At the Opening of a School in Kingswood." Italics added for emphasis.

of God. Christ alone is the key to participation in the divine nature. Hence, his birth, passion, death, resurrection, and ascension are the central foci of participation. Wesley's approach to participation in the divine nature is unequivocally christological. Here he is in concert with Kallistos Ware's comments: "The process of deification cannot be considered apart from the person of Christ. It is not a metaphysical, or neoplatonic, deification. It is operated through the Sacred Humanity of our Lord. The Incarnate Christ remains the Alpha and the Omega of our spiritual life."[19]

Participation transpires only through God's indwelling of individuals, which is initiated by the gift of the Holy Spirit at baptism and the participation in Christ's body and blood at Holy Communion. Thus, God dwells within us, and throughout our lives we are gradually "conformed to the image of his Son" (Rom 8:29). In the Wesleyan view this transpires through acts of piety and acts of mercy. Our life in the triune God is enriched through prayer, meditation, study, observance of the means of grace, and the practice of acts of charity, especially outreach to the poor. These practices lead toward maturity in the image of Christ and are requisite to participation in the divine nature, which is enabled solely through the grace of God. Furthermore, acts of piety and acts of mercy are an integral part of the sacramental path of participation.

Charles Wesley does not flesh out distinctions between divine image and divine likeness, though he does emphasize that the divine image is a key to the understanding of participation in the divine nature. For him image and likeness are almost synonyms. Here is a difference with the teaching of many church fathers for whom the distinction between image and likeness is central to the understanding of *theosis*, for one moves from the divine image to the divine likeness.

For Charles Wesley participation does not make of us something that we are not. It does not nullify our humanness. "This is precisely the point that Maximus is making about mystical assumption: that it confers the gift of deification, of true participation in the deity of Christ, but does not in the process obliterate humanity. And that, in turn, is the full meaning of the Athanasian principle: 'He [the Logos] was made man that we might be made God,' but not at the price of our own most authentic selves."[20] Through participation in the divine nature and receiving its power our humanity becomes truly authentic. We are then the persons God intends

19. A Monk of the Eastern Church, *Orthodox Spirituality*, 99.
20. Pelikan, "Christian Mysticism East and West," 6.

for us to be. By growing into the mature image of Christ, we share in the life of the Holy Trinity and the divine nature, which is love. Fulfillment in divine love, which transforms our being and every aspect of our behavior, is the ultimate divine gift of participation. This transformation means that participation in the divine nature is a gift of grace and a way of life.

> To live theosis, then, means to lead our life in an eschatological perspective within the ecclesial community, striving through prayer, participation in the Eucharist, and the practice of the moral life to attain the divine likeness, being conformed spiritually and corporeally to the body of Christ until we are brought into Christ's identity and arrive ultimately at union with the Father.[21]

Conclusion

How shall we see Charles Wesley then in relationship to Orthodoxy and Orthodox theology? Elsewhere I have written an essay titled "Charles Wesley and a Window to the East"[22] in which I have annotated bibliographical sources that address significant ways in which his theology and praxis intersect with the churches of the East and the church fathers. In conclusion, it is worth noting a few such sources, which complement the emphasis on deification in this volume.

The study titled "From Glory to Glory: The Renewal of All Things in Christ"[23] is an examination by Kenneth Carveley of parallel theological ideas on deification and "religion of the heart" in St. Maximus the Confessor and the Wesley brothers. "Carveley's study emphasizes that both traditions, Orthodox and Wesleyan, more than advocating a set of doctrines, emphasize a way of life, a way of dynamic living with, in and through the Triune God."[24]

In "Charles Wesley and the Orthodox Hesychastic Tradition,"[25] Father Ioann Ekonomstev finds striking similarities between the poetry of Charles Wesley and St. Symeon the New Theologian and stresses that Charles's

---

21. Russell, *Fellow Workers with God*, 169.
22. In Newport and Campbell, *Charles Wesley: Life, Literature & Legacy*, 165–83.
23. In Kimbrough, *Orthodox and Wesleyan Spirituality*, ch. 9.
24. Kimbrough, "Charles Wesley and a Window to the East," 167.
25. In Kimbrough, *Orthodox and Wesleyan Spirituality*, ch. 12.

idea of participation in the divine creative energy makes him an important spiritual link between East and West.

Karen Westerfield Tucker, in her essay "The Liturgical Functioning of Orthodox Troparia and Wesleyan Hymns," explores similarities and differences of musical performance practice in the Orthodox and Wesleyan traditions. She finds common metaphors, images, and biblical language, and a shared hermeneutical principle: both traditions "read the story of the old covenant through the lens of the new."[26]

While Gordon S. Wakefield is primarily concerned with John Wesley's relationship to the Eastern Church in his article "John Wesley and Ephraem Syrus," he includes a brief discussion of Charles and avers, "It is above all in the [Wesleyan] hymns that theosis has its place in Methodism. And it is related to the Incarnation."[27]

In an article titled "Wesley Hymns: The Icons of the Wesleyan Tradition,"[28] I have explored a common thread of spiritual art in Orthodoxy and the Wesleys, namely, the creation of icons and poetry. In both instances the spiritual art forms that characterize these two traditions emerge from fasting, prayer, meditation, and the Eucharist.

> Contrasting visual art and verbal pictures painted with words, one finds amazing similarities between the Orthodox icon and the Wesleyan hymn. Just as the icons of the Eastern churches are windows to God and spirituality, so the Wesley hymns are windows through which to glimpse the way of holiness, to interpret faith and practice, to celebrate the saints, to explore the mystery of God, and to approach God.[29]

We can say unequivocally of this eighteenth-century Anglican poet/priest that he has the window to the East not partially open, but rather wide open. His theology of participation in the divine nature can serve as a vital bridge between West and East perhaps more effectively today than in the eighteenth century, since we now have the benefit of the full spectrum of his work. Furthermore, participation is not just another theological dimension of Charles Wesley's theology. This study reveals it to be a dominant dimension of his theology from which the other aspects of his theology flow.

---

26. Tucker, "Liturgical Functioning," 300.
27. Wakefield, "John Wesley and Ephraem Syrus," 280.
28. Kimbrough, "Wesley Hymns."
29. Kimbrough, "Charles Wesley and a Window to the East," 170.

Epilogue: The *Philokalia* and the Charles Wesley Corpus

The spiritual and theological revival associated with a group of monks from Mount Athos in Greece that emerged in the second half of the eighteenth century is well known in the history of the Eastern Church and, of course, to many theologians in the East and West. Among many other things, the group advocated frequent eucharistic participation. Two of the monks, Makarios of Corinth (1731–1805) and Nicodemus the Hagiorite (1749–1809), are thought to be the editors of a large collection of texts published in Venice, Italy, under the title *Philokalia* in 1782.[1]

"As an influential collection of texts, the *Philokalia* may be said to be a 'hermeneutical filter' which conditions the self-understanding of the Orthodox as well as the perception by the 'non-Orthodox' . . . The collection is offered to all Christians: monks and laity as 'a mystical school of noetic prayer.'"[2]

Is this not in some measure what one has in the Charles Wesley corpus of more than nine thousand hymns and poems plus his *MSJ*, sermons, and letters, namely, a "hermeneutical filter" that conditions the self-understanding of those affiliated with the Wesleyan movement, Anglicans and Methodists, and many other denominations that have been influenced by the Wesleys and particularly the hymns of Charles? In one sense they too are a corpus of mentally engaging prayer, since so many of the hymns were composed as prayers.

The closest one came in the lifetime of John and Charles Wesley to organizing the hymns into something of a "systematic" theological scheme was John Wesley's 1780 *Collection*, which organized more than five hundred Wesley hymns and a few by other authors as an *ordo salutis*, providing

---

1. See Collins, *Partaking in Divine Nature*, 88–91.
2. Ibid., 91. Collins quotes Ware, "Inner Unity," 12.

spiritual direction for the life of the Christian from birth in Christ to death, resurrection, and eternal life.

Although the number of Charles Wesley's hymns and poems that address the idea of participation in the divine nature is quite extensive, generally they have not received primary interest, either in organized collections or within the Wesleyan movement.

Now that Charles Wesley's extensive corpus of hymns and poems,[3] journal,[4] and sermons[5] are available for critical study, one hopes that many dimensions of his theology will be carefully explored.[6] Since his theology of participation in the divine nature is at the core of his theology, perhaps scholars of the East and West will examine this aspect of his literature more thoroughly in the future. Perhaps they will discover that his theology is an interesting and important bridge between East and West.

---

3. See the website of the Center for Studies in the Wesleyan Tradition of The Divinity School of Duke University, which includes all of the extant published and manuscript poetry of Charles Wesley: http://www.divinity.duke.edu/initiatives-centers/cswt/wesley-texts.

4. Kimbrough and Newport, *The Manuscript Journal of The Reverend Charles Wesley*.

5. Newport, *The Sermons of Charles Wesley*.

6. The publication of the large number of extant letters by Charles Wesley is currently in process. Their availability will be a valuable source for scholarly study. One volume of the letters has been published: Newport and Lloyd, *The Letters of Charles Wesley*, Vol. 1, 1728–1756.

Selected Bibliography

Allchin, A. M. *The Kingdom of Love and Knowledge: The Encounter between Orthodoxy and the West.* London: Darton, Longman & Todd, 1979.
———. *Participation in God: A Forgotten Strand in Anglican Tradition.* Wilton, CT: Morehouse-Barlow, 1988.
———. "The Trinity in the Teaching of Charles Wesley." *Proceedings of The Charles Wesley Society* 4 (1997) 69–84.
Andrewes, Lancelot. *Ninety-six Sermons.* Vol. 1, *Sermons of the Nativity and of Repentance and Fasting.* Library of Anglo-Catholic Theology. Oxford: J. H. Parker, 1841.
Arseniev, Nicholas. *Mysticism and the Eastern Church.* Translated by Arthur Chambers. Crestwood, NY: St. Vladimir's Seminary Press, 1979.
Athanasius, St. *Contra Gentes and De Incarnatione.* Edited and translated by Robert W. Thomson. Oxford Early Christian Texts. Oxford: Clarendon, 1971.
Baker, Frank, ed. *Representative Verse of Charles Wesley.* London: Epworth, 1962.
Baker, Frank, compiler. *A Union Catalogue of the Publications of John and Charles Wesley.* Durham: The Divinity School, Duke University, 1966.
Balás, David L. *Μετουσία Θεοῦ. Man's Participation in God's Perfections according to Saint Gregory of Nyssa.* Studia Anselmiana 55. Rome: Liebreria Herder, 1966.
Balthasar, Hans Urs von. *Présence et pensée. Essai sur la philosophie de Grégoire de Nysse.* Paris: Beauchesne, 1942.
Basil, St. *Doctrina patrum de incarnatione verbi.* Edited by Franz Diekamp. 2nd ed. Münster: Aschendorff, 1981.
Bigger, Charles P. *Participation: A Platonic Inquiry.* Baton Rouge: Louisiana State University, 1968.
Bilaniuk, P. B. T. "The Mystery of Theosis or Divinisation." In *The Heritage of the Early Church: Essays in Honor of Georges Vasilievich Florovsky*, edited by David Neiman and Margaret Schatkin, 337–59. Orientalia Christiana analecta 195. Rome: Pontificium Institutum Orientalium Studiorum, 1973.
Book of Common Prayer, 1549: Commonly Called the First Book of Edward VI. With an Introduction by Morgan Dix. New York: Church Kalendar Press, 1881.
Booty, John E. "Commentary." In vol. 6, Part 2 of *The Folger Library Edition of the Works of Richard Hooker*, edited by W. Speed Hill et al., 653–832. Binghamton, NY: Medieval and Renaissance Texts and Studies, 1993.
———. "Introduction to Book V." In vol. 6, Part 1 of *The Folger Library Edition of the Works of Richard Hooker*, edited by W. Speed Hill et al., 183–231. Binghamton, NY: Medieval and Renaissance Texts and Studies, 1993.
Bornhäuser, K. *Die Vergöttungslehre des Athansius und Johannes Damascenus.* Beiträge zur Förderung christlicher Theologie 2. Gütersloh: C. Bertelsmann, 1903.

Selected Bibliography

Bowmer, John C. *The Sacrament of the Lord's Supper in Early Methodism.* London: Dacre, 1951.
Braaten, Carl E., and Robert W. Jenson, eds. *Union with Christ: The New Finnish Interpretation of Luther.* Grand Rapids: Eerdmans, 1998.
Brock, Sebastian. "An Early Syriac Life of Maximus the Confessor." *Analecta Bolladiana* 91 (1973) 299–346.
———, trans. *The Syriac Fathers on the Spiritual Life.* Cistercian Studies Series 101. Kalamazoo, MI: Cistercian Publications, 1987.
Burghardt, Walter J. *The Image of God in Man according to Cyril of Alexandria.* Washington, DC: Catholic University of America Press, 1957.
Butterworth, G. W. "The Deification of Man in Clement of Alexandria." *Journal of Theological Studies* 17 (1916) 157–69.
Campbell, Ted A. *John Wesley and Christian Antiquity: Religious Vision and Cultural Change.* Nashville: Kingswood, 1991.
Charlesworth, James Hamilton, ed. and trans. *The Odes of Solomon.* Oxford: Clarendon, 1973.
Cherniss, Harold Fredrik. *The Platonism of Gregory of Nyssa.* New York: B. Franklin, 1971.
Christensen, Michael J. "John Wesley: Christian Perfection as Faith Filled with the Energy of Love." In *Partakers of the Divine Nature*, edited by Michael J. Christensen and Jeffrey A. Wittung, 219–29. Madison, NJ: Fairleigh Dickinson University Press, 2007.
———. "*Theosis* and Sanctification: John Wesley's Reformulation of a Patristic Doctrine." *Wesleyan Theological Journal* 31 (1996) 71–94.
Christensen, Michael J., and Jeffrey A. Wittung, eds. *Partakers of the Divine Nature.* Madison, NJ: Fairleigh Dickinson University Press, 2007.
Clement of Alexandria. *The Seventh Book of the Stromateis.* Edited by Matyáš Havrda et al. Leiden: Brill, 2012.
Climacus, John, St. *The Ladder of Divine Ascent.* Translated by Archimandrite Lazarus Moore. New York: Harper, 1959.
Cocksworth, Christopher J. *Evangelical Eucharistic Thought in the Church of England.* Cambridge: Cambridge University Press, 1993.
Collins, Paul M. *Partaking in Divine Nature: Deification and Communion.* London: T. & T. Clark, 2010.
Congar, M.-J. "La deification dans la tradition spirituelle de l'Orient." *La Vie Spirituelle* 43, supplement 91–107, 1935. Reprinted in *Unam Sanctam* 50, Paris, 1964.
Cooper, Adam G. *The Body in St. Maximus the Confessor.* Oxford: Oxford University Press, 2005.
Cornwall, Robert D. "The Later Nonjurors and the Theological Basis of the Usages Controversy." *Anglican Theological Review* 75 (1993) 166–86.
Cyril, Patriarch of Alexandria, St. *Commentary on the Gospel according to John.* Vol. 1, *S. John I–VIII.* Translated by P. E. Pusey. Oxford: James Parker, 1874.
Danielou, Jean. *Platonisme et théologie mystique: Essai sur la doctrine spirituelle de saint Gregoire de Nysse.* 2nd ed. Paris: Aubier, 1954.
Drewery, Ben. "Deification." In *Christian Spirituality: Essays in Honour of Gordon Rupp*, edited by Peter Brooks, 33–62. London: SCM, 1975.
Ellverson, Anna-Stina. *The Dual Nature of Man: A Study in the Theological Anthropology of Gregory of Nazianzus.* Uppsala: Almqvist & Wiksell, 1981.
Ephrem, Syrus, St. *Ephrem the Syrian: Hymns.* Translated by Kathleen E. McVey. Classics of Western Spirituality. New York: Paulist, 1989.

Selected Bibliography

———. *Hymns on Paradise*. Translated by Sebastian Brock. Crestwood, NY: St. Vladimir's Seminary Press, 1990.

Every, George. "Theosis in Later Byzantine Theology." *Eastern Churches Review* 2 (1969) 243–52.

Finch, Jeffrey D. "Neo-Palamism, Divinizing Grace, and the Breach between East and West." In *Partakers of the Divine Nature*, edited by Michael J. Christiansen and Jeffrey A. Wittung, 233–49. Madison, NJ: Fairleigh Dickinson University Press, 2007.

George, Archimandrite. *Theosis: The True Purpose of Human Life*. Mount Athos: Holy Monastery of St. Gregorios, 2006.

Golitzin, Alexander. *On the Mystical Life: The Ethical Discourses*. Vol. 3, *Life, Times, and Theology*. Crestwood, NY: St. Vladimir's Seminary Press, 1996.

Gross, Jules. *La divinization du chrétien d'après les Pères grecs*. Paris: Gabalda, 1938. Translated by Paul A. Onica. *The Divinization of the Christian according to the Greek Fathers*. Anaheim, CA: A & C, 2002.

Habets, Myk. "Reforming Theōsis." In *Theosis: Deification in Christian Theology*, edited by Stephen Finlan and Vladimir Kharlamov, 146–67. Eugene, OR: Pickwick, 2006.

Heitzenrater, Richard P. "John Wesley's Reading of and References to the Early Church Fathers." In *Orthodox and Wesleyan Spirituality*, edited by S T Kimbrough, Jr., 25–31. Crestwood, NY: St. Vladimir's Seminary Press, 2002.

———. *Wesley and the People Called Methodists*. Nashville: Abingdon, 1995.

Hooker, Richard. *The Works of Richard Hooker . . . in Eight Books of Ecclesiastical Polity*. London: Printed by Thomas Newcomb for Andrew Crooke, 1666.

Hotchkiss, Valerie, and Patrick Henry, eds. *Orthodoxy and Western Culture: A Collection of Essays Honoring Jaroslav Pelikan on his Eightieth Birthday*. Crestwood, NY: St. Vladimir's Seminary Press, 2005.

Hudson, Nancy J. *Becoming God: The Doctrine of Theosis in Nicholas of Cusa*. Washington, DC: Catholic University of America Press, 2007.

Jaeger, W. *Gregor von Nyssas Lehre vom Heiligen Geist*. Edited by H. Dörries. Leiden: Brill, 1966.

Jensen, Chris. "Shine as the Sun: C. S. Lewis and the Doctrine of Deification; The Orthodox Worldview and C. S. Lewis (Part II)." *Road to Emmaus* 8 (2007) 40–62.

Kärkkäinen, Veli-Matti. *One with God: Salvation as Deification and Justification*. Collegeville, MN: Liturgical, 2004.

Kalaitzidis, Pantelis. "The West in Contemporary Greek Theology." In *Orthodox Constructions of the West*, edited by G. Demacopoulos and A. Papanikolaou, 142–60. New York: Fordham University Press, 2013.

Keating, Daniel A. *The Appropriation of Divine Life in Cyril of Alexandria*. Oxford: Oxford University Press, 2004.

———. *Deification and Grace*. Naples, FL: Sapientia, 2007.

Kharlamov, Vladimir. "Rhetorical Application of *Theosis* in Greek Patristic Theology." In *Partakers of the Divine Nature*, edited by Michael J. Christiansen and Jeffrey A. Wittung, 115–31. Madison, NJ: Fairleigh Dickinson University Press, 2007.

Kimbrough, S T, Jr. "Charles Wesley and a Window to the East." In *Charles Wesley: Life, Literature & Legacy*, edited by Kenneth G. C. Newport and Ted A. Campbell, 165–83. Peterborough: Epworth, 2007.

———. "Charles Wesley and Slavery." *Proceedings of The Charles Wesley Society* 13 (2009) 35–52.

Selected Bibliography

———. "Charles Wesley's Understanding of the Nature of the Church." In *Orthodox and Wesleyan Ecclesiology*, edited by S T Kimbrough, Jr., 129–47. Crestwood, NY, 2002.

———, ed. *Orthodox and Wesleyan Scriptural Understanding and Practice*. Crestwood, NY: St. Vladimir's Seminary Press, 2005.

———, ed. *Orthodox and Wesleyan Spirituality*. Crestwood, NY: St. Vladimir's Seminary Press, 2002.

———, ed. *Songs of the Poor: Hymns*. New York: General Board of Global Ministries, United Methodist Church, 1993.

———. "*Theosis* in the Writings of Charles Wesley." *St. Vladimir's Theological Quarterly* 52 (2008) 199–212.

———. "Wesley Hymns: The Icons of the Wesleyan Tradition." *Proceedings of The Charles Wesley Society* 8 (2002) 24–40.

Kirov, Dimitar. "The Mysticism of Light." In *Orthodox and Wesleyan Scriptural Understanding and Practice*, edited by S T Kimbrough, Jr., 117–26. Crestwood, NY: St. Vladimir's Seminary Press, 2005.

———. "The Unity of Revelation and the Unity of Tradition." In *Orthodox and Wesleyan Scriptural Understanding and Practice*, edited by S T Kimbrough, Jr., 105–17. Crestwood, NY: St. Valdimir's Seminary Press, 2007.

Klostermann, Erich, and Heinz Berthold, eds. *The Homilies of St. Macarius*. 3rd ed. Texte und Untersuchungen 72. Berlin: Akademie-Verlag, 1961.

Koder, Johannes, ed. *Hymnes*. Translated by Joseph Paramelle. 3 vols. Paris: Cerf, 1969–73.

Kolp, A. L. "Partakers of the Divine Nature: The Use of II Peter 1:4 by Athanasius." *Studia Patristica* 17 (1982) 1018–23.

Krivocheine, B. "Essence créée et essence divine dans la théologie spirituelle de S. Syméon le nouveau théologien." *Messager de l'Exarchat du Patriarche Russe en Europe Occidental* 75–76 (1971) 151–70.

Larchet, Jean-Claude. *La divinisation de l'homme selon saint Maxime le Confesseur*. Cogitato Fidei 194. Paris: Cerf, 1996.

Lattey, C. "The Deification of Man in Clement of Alexandria: Some Further Notes." *Journal of Theological Studies* 17 (1916) 257–62.

Lawson, John. *The Biblical Theology of Saint Irenaeus*. London: Epworth, 1948.

Lossky, Nicholas. "Lancelot Andrewes: A Bridge between Orthodoxy and the Wesley Brothers in the Realm of Prayer." In *Orthodox and Wesleyan Spirituality: Scriptural Understanding and Practice*, edited by S T Kimbrough, Jr., 149–56. Crestwood, NY: St. Vladimir's Seminary Press, 2005.

———. *Lancelot Andrewes the Preacher (1555–1625): The Origins of the Mystical Theology of the Church of England*. Translated by Andrew Louth. Oxford: Clarendon, 1991.

Lossky, Vladimir. *In the Image and Likeness of God*. Crestwood, NY: St. Vladimir's Seminary Press, 1974.

———. *The Mystical Theology of the Eastern Church*. Cambrdige: James Clarke, 1991.

———. *Orthodox Theology: An Introduction*. Translated by Ian and Ihita Kesarcodi-Watson. Crestwood, NY: St. Vladimir's Seminary Press, 1978.

Louth, Andrew. "Manhood into God: The Oxford Movement, the Fathers and the Deification of Man." In *Essays Catholic and Radical*, edited by Kenneth Leech and Rowan Williams, 70–80. London: Bowerdean, 1983.

———. *Maximus the Confessor*. London: Routledge, 1996.

Selected Bibliography

Loyer, Kenneth M. "Memorial, Means, and Pledge: Eucharist and Time in the Wesleys' Hymns on the Lord's Supper." *Proceedings of The Charles Wesley Society* 11 (2006-7) 87-106.
Nicodemus the Hagiorite, St. *Nicodemos of the Holy Mountain: A Handbook of Spiritual Counsel.* Translated by Peter A. Chamberas. New York: Paulist, 1989.
Maddox, Randy A. "John Wesley and Eastern Orthodoxy: Influences, Convergences, and Differences." *Asbury Theological Journal* 45 (1990) 29-53.
———. *Responsible Grace: John Wesley's Practical Theology.* Nashville: Kingswood, 1994.
Maloney, George A. *Gold, Frankincense, and Myrrh: An Introduction to Eastern Christian Spirituality.* New York: Crossroad, 1997.
Mantzaridis, G. I. *The Deification of Man: St. Gregory Palamas and the Orthodox Tradition.* Translated by by Liadain Sherrard. Crestwood, NY: St. Vladimir's Seminary Press, 1997.
Mascall, E. L. *Christ, the Christian and the Church: A Study of the Incarnation and Its Consequences.* London: Longmans, Green, 1946.
Maximus, Confessor, St. *Four Hundred Texts on Love.* In vol. 2 of *The Philokalia*, translated and edited by G. E. H. Palmer et al., 64-155. London: Faber & Faber, 1981.
Mayer, A. *Das Gottesbild im Menschen nach Clemens von Alexandrien.* Studia Anselmiana 15. Rome: Herder, 1942.
McAdoo, Henry Robert. "A Theology of the Eucharist: Brevint and the Wesleys." *Theology* 97 (1994) 245-56.
McAdoo, Henry Robert, and Kenneth Stevenson. *The Mystery of the Eucharist in the Anglican Tradition.* Norwich: Canterbury, 1995.
McCormick, Steve K. "Theosis in Chrysostom and Wesley: An Eastern Paradigm of Faith and Love." *Wesleyan Theological Journal* 26 (1991) 38-103.
McGuckin, John A. *Saint Gregory of Nazianzus: An Intellectual Biography.* Crestwood, NY: St. Vladimir's Seminary Press, 1986.
———. "The Strategic Adaptation of Deification in the Cappadocians." In *Partakers of the Divine Nature*, edited by Michael J. Christiansen and Jeffrey A. Wittung, 95-114. Madison, NJ: Fairleigh Dickinson University Press, 2007.
Meistad, Tore. "The Missiology of Charles Wesley and Its Links to the Eastern Church." In *Orthodox and Wesleyan Spirituality*, edited by S T Kimbrough, Jr., 205-31. Crestwood, NY: St. Vladimir's Seminary Press, 2002.
Meredith, Anthony. *Gregory of Nyssa.* London: Routledge, 1999.
Meyendorff, John. *Byzantine Theology.* New York: Fordham University Press, 1974.
———. *A Study of Gregory Palamas.* Translated by George Lawrence. London: Faith Press, 1964.
———. "Theosis in the Eastern Christian Tradition." In *Christian Spirituality: Post-Reformation and Modern*, edited by Louis Dupré et al., 470-76. New York: Crossroad, 1989.
Migne, J.-P., ed. *Patrologia graeca.* 161 vols. Paris, 1857-66.
A Monk of the Eastern Church. *Orthodox Spirituality: An Outline of the Orthodox Ascetical and Mystical Tradition.* 2nd ed. Crestwood, NY: St. Vladimir's Seminary Press, 1996.
Mosser, Carl. "The Earliest Patristic Interpretation of Psalm 82, Jewish Antecedent, and the Origins of Christian Deification." *Journal of Theological Studies*, n.s., 56 (2005) 30-74.
———. "The Greatest Possible Blessing: Calvin and Deification." *Scottish Journal of Theology* 55 (2002) 36-57.

Selected Bibliography

Nellas, Panayiotis. *Deification in Christ: Orthodox Perspectives on the Nature of the Human Person*. Translated by Norman Russell. Crestwood, NY: St. Vladimir's Seminary Press, 1997.

Newman, John Henry. *Lectures on Justification*. Oxford: J. H. Parker, 1838.

Newport, Kenneth G. C., ed. *The Sermons of Charles Wesley: A Critical Edition with Introduction and Notes*. Oxford, UK: Oxford University Press, 2001.

Newport, Kenneth G. C. and Gareth Lloyd, eds. *The Letters of Charles Wesley. Vol. 1, 1728–1756*. Oxford, UK: Oxford University Press, 2013.

Newport, Kenneth G. C., and Ted A. Campbell, eds. *Charles Wesley: Life, Literature & Legacy*. Peterborough: Epworth, 2007.

Outler, Albert C., ed. *John Wesley*. Oxford: Oxford University Press, 1964.

Papademetriou, George C. *Introduction to Saint Gregory Palamas*. New York: Philosophical Library, 1973.

Patterson, L. G. "The Divine Became Human: Irenaean Themes in Clement of Alexandria." *Studia Patristica* 31 (1997) 497–516.

Pelikan, Jaroslav. "Christian Mysticism East and West." James I. McCord Memorial Lectures, Fall 1990. *Reports from the Center, Number 4*, 1–15. Princeton: Center of Theological Inquiry, 1991.

Pseudo-Macarius. *The Fifty Spiritual Homilies and the "Great Letter"*. Translated and edited by George A. Maloney. Classics of Western Spirituality. New York: Paulist, 1992.

Pusey, Edward Bouverie. *The Holy Eucharist a Comfort to the Penitent: A Sermon Preached Before the University in the Cathedral Church of Christ in Oxford on the Fourth Sunday after Easter*. Oxford: J. H. Parker, 1843.

Quantrille, Wilma J. "The Triune God in the Hymns of Charles Wesley." PhD diss., Drew University, 1989.

Rakestraw, Robert V. "Becoming like God: An Evangelical Doctrine of Theosis." *Journal of Evangelical Theology* 40 (1996) 411–28.

Rattenbury, J. Ernest. *The Eucharistic Hymns of John and Charles Wesley*. London: Epworth, 1948.

Russell, Norman. *The Doctrine of Deification in the Greek Patristic Tradition*. Oxford: Oxford University Press, 2004.

———. *Fellow Workers with God: Orthodox Thinking on Theosis*. Crestwood, NY: St. Vladimir's Seminary Press, 2009.

———. "Partakers of the Divine Nature (2 Peter 1:4) in the Byzantine Tradition." In *Kathēgētria: Essays Presented to Joan Hussey on Her 80th Birthday*, edited by J. Chrysostomides, 51–67. Camberley: Porphyrogenitus, 1988.

Savvidis, Kyriakos. *Die Lehre von der Vergöttlichung des Menschen bei Maximos dem Bekenner und ihre Rezeption durch Gregor Palamas*. Veröffentlichung des Instituts für Orthodoxe Theologie 5. St. Ottilien: EOS, 1997.

Scougal, Henry. *The Life of God in the Soul of Man*. Edited by Winthrop S. Hudson. Philadelphia: Westminster, 1948.

Schaff, Philip and Henry Wace, eds. *Nicene and Post-Nicene Fathers of the Christian Church*, Second series. 14 vols. Reprint. Peabody, MA: Hendrickson, 1994.

Seraphim of Sarov, St. *Concerning the Aim of the Christian Life*. Translated by A. F. Dobbie-Bateman. London: SPCK, 1936.

Stamoolis, J. *Eastern Orthodox Mission Theology Today*. Maryknoll, NY: Orbis, 1986.

Selected Bibliography

Stăniloae, Dumitru. *Orthodox Spirituality*. Translated by Archimandrite Jerome (Newville) and Otilia Kloos. South Canaan, PA: St. Tikhon's Seminary Press, 2002.
Starr, James M. *Sharers in Divine Nature: 2 Peter 1:4 in Its Hellenistic Context*. Coniectanea Biblica New Testament Series 33. Stockholm: Almqvist & Wiksell, 2000.
Stavropoulos, Christoforos. *Partakers of the Divine Nature*. Translated by Stanley Harakas. Minneapolis: Light and Life, 1976.
Stevick, Daniel. *The Altar's Fire: Charles Wesley's Hymns on the Lord's Supper, 1745: Introduction and Exposition*. Peterborough: Epworth, 2004.
Strange, C. R. "Athanasius on Divinization." *Studia Patristica* 16 (1985) 342–46.
Symeon, the New Theologian, St. *Hymns of Divine Love*. Translated by George A. Maloney. Denville, NJ: Dimenson Books, 1976.
Taft, Robert J. "The Epiclesis Question in the Light of the Orthodox and Catholic *Lex Orandi* Traditions." In *New Perspectives on Historical Theology: Essays in Memory of John Meyendorff*, edited by B. Nassif, 210–37. Grand Rapids: Eerdmans, 1996.
Tucker, Karen B. Westerfield. "The Liturgical Functioning of Orthodox Troparia and Wesleyan Hymns." In *Orthodox and Wesleyan Scriptural Understanding and Practice*, edited by S T Kimbrough, Jr., 293–304. Crestwood, NY: St. Vladimir's Seminary Press, 2005.
Vassiliadis, Petrus. *Eucharist and Witness: Orthodox Perspectives on the Unity and Mission of the Church*. Geneva: World Council of Churches, 1998.
Wainwright, Geoffrey. *Eucharist and Eschatology*. London: Epworth, 1971.
———. "'Our Elder Brethren Join': The Patristic Revival in England." *Proceedings of The Charles Wesley Society* 1 (1994) 5–31.
———. "Trinitarian Theology and Wesleyan Holiness." In *Orthodox and Wesleyan Spirituality*, edited by S T Kimbrough, Jr., 59–80. Crestwood, NY: St. Vladimir's Seminary Press, 2002.
Wakefield, Gordon S. "Charles Wesley's Spirituality and Its Meaning for Today." *The Charles Wesley Society Newsletter* 3 (1993) 3–25; *Proceedings of The Charles Wesley Society* 18 (2014) 79–99.
———. "John Wesley and Ephraem Syrus." *Hygoye: Journal of Syriac Studies* 1 (1998) 273–86.
Ware, Kallistos. "Deification in St Symeon the New Theologian." *Sobornost* 25 (2003) 7–29.
———. *The Orthodox Church*. London: Penguin, 1964.
———. *The Orthodox Way*. Crestwood, NY: St. Vladimir's Seminary Press, 1998.
———. "Salvation and Theosis in Orthodox Theology." In *Luther et la réforme allemande dans une perspective oecuménique*, edited by W. Schneemelcher, 167–84. Geneva: Éditions du Centre Orthodoxe, 1983.
Weinandy, Thomas G. "St. Irenaeus and the *Imago Dei*." *Logos* 6 (2003) 15–34.
Wesche, Kenneth Paul. "Eastern Orthodox Spirituality: Union with God in *Theosis*." *Theology Today* 56 (1999) 29–43.
Wesley, Charles. *The Letters of Charles Wesley. Vol. 1, 1728–1756*. Edited by Kenneth G. C. Newport and Gareth Lloyd. Oxford: Oxford University Press, 2013.
———. *The Manuscript Journal of the Rev. Charles Wesley, M. A. 2 vols*. Edited by S T Kimbrough, Jr., and Kenneth G. C. Newport. Nashville: Kingswood, 2008.
———. *The Sermons of Charles Wesley*. Edited by Kenneth G. C. Newport. Oxford: Oxford University Press, 2001.

Selected Bibliography

Wesley, John. *John Wesley's Sunday Service of Methodists in North America*. Nashville: United Methodist Publishing House and the United Methodist Board of Higher Education and Ministry, 1984.

Williams, A. N. *The Ground of Union: Deification in Aquinas and Palamas*. Oxford: Oxford University Press, 1999.

Williams, Rowan. "Deification." In *A Dictionary of Christian Spirituality*, edited by Gordon S. Wakefield, 106–8. London: SCM, 1983.

Yannaras, Christos. *Elements of Faith: An Introduction to Orthodox Theology*. Translated by Keith Schram. Edinburgh: T. & T. Clark, 1991.

Index of Personal Names

Acquinas, St. Thomas, 43
Adam, 46, 51, 67, 74, 129
Allchin, A. M., 2, 4–6, 8–9, 27, 37, 61, 141, 151
Ambrose, of Milan St., 6, 43
Andrewes, Lancelot, x, 5–6, 8–9, 17, 136–37, 141–42, 151, 154
Ashanin, Charles B., 126
Athanasius of Alexander, St., 6, 12, 26, 38, 40, 43, 46, 51, 60, 69, 141, 151, 154, 157
Augustine, St., 6, 43
Basil the Great, St., 14–15, 47, 51, 56, 110, 139, 141, 151
Bell, George, 124
Bernard of Clairvaux, St., 142–43
Berthold, Heinz, 154
Booty, John E., 6, 151
Bowmer, John C., 58, 152
Braaten, Carl E., 4, 152
Calvin, John, 4, 43, 155
Campbell, Ted A., 3, 17, 146, 152–53, 156
Carveley, Kenneth, 146
Causse, Antonin, 3
Charlesworth, James, 106, 152
Cherniss, Harold, 143, 152
Christensen, Michael J., 4, 8, 152
Chrysostom, St. John, 4, 6, 43, 51, 56, 77, 80, 99, 155–56
Clement of Alexandria, St., 7, 137–38, 152, 154, 156
Climacus, St. John, 73, 152
Collins, Paul M., 4–5, 7, 130, 138, 140–42, 149, 152

Cooper, Adam G., 142, 152
Cranmer, Thomas, 55
Cyprian, St., 6
Cyril of Alexandria, St., 4, 7, 49, 52, 60, 69, 71–72, 107, 139, 152–53
Cyril of Jerusalem, St., 22
Danielou, Jean, 143, 152
Deacon, Thomas, 50–51, 56–57
Delamotte, Mrs, 16–18
Dionysius, St., 50, 139
Dobbie-Bateman, A. F., 156
Drewery, Ben, 8, 152
Durkheim, Emile, 3
Ekonomstev, Ioann, 146
Elias, 113, 115,
Ephrem the Syrian, xii, 7, 38–39, 43, 51, 94, 134, 136, 138, 152
Finch, Jeffrey D., 14, 153
George, Archimandrite, 3, 37, 86, 153
Golitzin, Alexander, 13, 20, 53, 84, 97, 103–4, 107, 153
Gregory of Nazianzus, St., xi, 2, 6–7, 43, 141, 152, 155
Gregory of Nyssa, St., 7, 18, 43, 47, 53, 94, 134, 141, 143, 151–52, 155
Heidegger, Martin, 1
Heitzenrater, Richard P., 3, 124, 153
Henry VIII, King, 84
Hilary of Poitiers, 43
Hooker, Richard, 4–6, 17, 136–37, 142, 151, 153
Horton, Mary, 109–10
Hudson, Nancy J., 71, 99, 153

Irenaeus, St., 6, 43, 91–92, 138, 154, 157
Isaac the Syrian, St., 94
Jacob, 88, 91
James, St., 56, 114, 120
Jenson, Robert W., 4, 152
Jerome, St., 6
John of Damascus, St., 43, 139
John, St., 114, 120
Jones, William, 61
Kärkkäinen, Veli-Matt, 4, 153
Keating, Daniel, 4, 43, 49, 52, 60, 69, 120, 153
Keble, John, 5
Kharlamov, Vladimir, 39–40, 61, 153
Kimbrough, S T, Jr., xi, xiv, 2, 4, 8, 77, 84, 97, 146–47, 150, 153–55, 157
Kirov, Dimitar, 39, 92, 154
Kishkovsky, Leonid, 50
Klostermann, Erich, 154
Koder, J., 11, 154
Krivocheine, B., 13, 154
Lessing, Gotthold Ephraim, 1
Lévy-Bruhl, Lucien, 3
Lossky, Nicholas, 5, 8, 154
Lossky, Vladimir, x, 13, 154
Louth, Andrew, 4, 39, 99, 154
Loyer, Kenneth M., 57, 155
Luther, Martin, 43, 152, 157
Macarius, St., 17, 105–6, 115, 154, 156
Maddox, Randy, 3, 126, 155
Makarios of Corinth, St., 149
Maloney, George A., 46, 121, 155–57
Mantzaridis, G. I., 4, 67, 155
Mascall, E. L., 4, 155
Maxfield, Thomas, 16, 124
Maximus, St. the Confessor, 2, 7, 12, 39, 43, 71, 99, 116, 136, 139, 141–42, 145–46, 152, 154
McCormick, Steve K., 4, 155
McGuckin, John, 19, 127, 155
McVey, Kathleen, 39, 152
Meistad, Tore, 126, 155
Meyendorff, John, 4, 7, 13–14, 46, 64, 155

Moses, 102, 113, 115–16
Mosser, Carl, 4, 137, 155
Nellas, Panayiotis, 50, 156
Newman, John Henry, 5, 156
Newport, Kenneth G. C., xiv, 146, 150, 153, 156–57
Nikodemos the Hagiorite, St. / Nicodemos of the Holy Mountain, 102, 149, 155
Origen, 2, 7, 69, 94, 134, 137, 139
Palamas, Gregory, 7, 13–15, 45–46, 67, 69, 120, 138, 155–56, 158
Pantycelyn, Williams, 5
Papademetrious, George C., 156
Paul, St., 33, 80, 124
Pelikan, Jaroslav, 145, 153
Peter, St., 102, 114, 117, 120
Pusey, Edward Bouverie, 5, 49, 52, 156
Quantrille, Wilma J., 61, 156
Rattenbury, J. Ernest, 59, 156
Robin John, Ancona, 84
Robin John, Ephraim, 84
Russell, Norman, 2, 4, 7, 18, 60, 69–70, 72, 86, 99, 105, 116, 120, 136, 140, 146, 156
Scougal, Henry, 17, 21, 136–37, 142, 156
Seraphim of Sarov, St., 11, 156
Stamoolis, J., 3–4, 156
Stăniloae, Dumitru, 131, 157
Symeon the New Theologian, St., xi, 9, 11–13, 15, 43, 53–54, 84, 96, 101, 103, 107, 126, 146, 154, 157
Taft, Robert, S. J., 55, 157
Tucker, Westerfield Karen, 147, 157
Wainwright, Geoffrey, 5, 50–51, 56, 65, 157
Wakefield, Gordon S., 3, 37–38, 140, 147, 157
Ware, Kallistos, 4, 13, 40, 59, 145, 149, 157
Weber, Max, 3
Wesley, Charles, xi–xii, xiv–xv, 1–20, 22–62, 64–88, 91–99, 101–2, 104–11, 113–18, 120–28,

  130–34, 136–47, 149–51,
  153–57
Wesley, John, xiv, 3, 5, 8, 17, 56–57,
  66, 123, 130, 142, 147, 149,
  152–53, 155–58
Wittgenstein, Ludwig, 1
Wittung, Jeffrey A., 152
Yannaras, Christos, 1–2, 158

Index of Scripture Passages

OLD TESTAMENT

Genesis
1:26,	72
2:23	82
32:24–32	88

Exodus
3:14	40
34:30	102

Leviticus
11:45	125

Numbers
6:24	62

Deuteronomy
7:7–8	9

Job
11:7	10

Psalms
51:10	92
81:6	137
82	137, 155

Proverbs
4:18	122

Song of Solomon
6:10	103

Isaiah
31:9	101
32:2	27
40:8	66, 104
61	106

Jeremiah
31:22	37
31:34	12

Ezekiel
37:3–4	13

Hosea
1:7	93
12:4	94

Joel
2:28	11

Zephaniah
3:14–15	95

NEW TESTAMENT

Matthew
5:3–12	97, 107
5:14	111
6:22	111
13:26f	123
17:3	113
17:4	102

Mark
4:26–27	130
4:28	124
9:2	114
9:3	119
9:4	115
9:5	117
9:6	117
9:7	118
9:8	114

Luke
8:56	69
9:28	120
9:31	119
9:35	116
11:2	65
12:50	98
17:21	21

John
1:12	32
1:12–14a	49
5:21	26
6:1	72
6:55–56	76
6:63	26
14:23	87
17:22	105

Acts of the Apostles
2	18
10:38	21
19:2	21
19:5	48
19:5–6	47
20:7	53

Romans
3:4	33
3:23–25	19
3:27	96
13:14	96
14:17	21

1 Corinthians
1:30	75
6:17	87
6:19	21
10:17	80
15:31	33

2 Corinthians
2:16	124
11:12	123
13:5	21

Galatians
2:16	124
4:19	21

Ephesians
1:13	21
1:14	21
4:30	21
5:14	20
5:30	109

Philippians
3:10	126
4:7	21

Colossians
1:27	21

1 Thessalonians

4:3	127
5:24	125

2 Thessalonians

1:4	34

2 Timothy

2:15	124

Hebrews

3:14	70

James

1:27	21
2:24	124
5:7	125

1 Peter

1:8	21

2 Peter

1:4	21, 69, 71, 136–37, 156–57
2:2	123

1 John

3:18	129
3:24	21
4:8	11, 88, 132
4:12, 15–16	87
4:20	99
5:10	21

Revelation of John

3:1–2	33, 34
3:4–5	110
3:12	102, 107

Index of Subjects

Anamnesis, 56
Angel(s), 10–11, 19, 34, 38, 43, 91, 94, 104, 110, 118
Anglicanism, 61, 155
   Anglican tradition, 8,
Antinomianism, 124
Apostolic Age, 47
Apostolic Constitutions, 50, 56
Arianism, 61
Articles of Religion, 138
Athanasian Creed, 26
Baptism, 41, 45–50
Beatitudes, 97, 107
Book of Common Prayer, xiv–xv, 26, 47, 50, 55, 92, 151
Cappadocians, 43, 155
Christology, 71, 143
Church Fathers, vii, x–xi, 2–3, 5–8, 15, 46, 48–50, 58, 73, 113–14, 116, 120, 134, 136–37, 139–40, 143, 145–46, 153
Church of England, xiv–xv, 1, 5, 19, 56, 61, 77, 107, 139, 142, 152, 154
Clementine liturgy, 50
Communion of saints, 67, 80, 96
Confirmation, 46
Creation, xi, 12, 19–20, 28–29, 66, 71–72, 79, 87, 110, 126, 136, 147
Death, xiii, 20, 33, 41, 46, 48, 58, 67–68, 70, 79, 84, 92, 94, 96, 100, 109, 116–17, 119–20, 138, 142, 145, 150

Deification, ix–xi, 2–5, 7–8, 15, 17, 19, 23, 32–33, 37–40, 43, 48–54, 58–60, 62, 64, 67, 69, 71, 74, 79, 85, 92, 94–96, 95, 99, 101, 104–5, 107–8, 110, 113, 115, 118–21, 126–28, 130–31, 134–46, 152–58
Divine energy, 13–15, 137
Divine essence, 7, 11, 13–15, 137, 141, 143
Divine image, 20, 45–46, 50, 62, 75, 95, 106–8, 133, 145
Divine light, 102, 108, 111, 114, 117
Divine likeness, 46, 138, 145–46
Divine nature, 1–7, 14, 16–26, 32, 37, 39–41, 44–45, 48, 50–53, 57–58, 60–62, 65–68, 70–71, 74–76, 81, 85, 87–88, 91, 96, 99, 101, 104–107, 113, 122, 126–28, 130–47, 149–50, 152–57
Eastern Church, 1, 4, 13, 39, 46, 55–56, 69, 98, 103, 107, 122, 127, 145, 147, 149, 151, 153–55
Ecclesiology, xi, 2, 22, 44, 46, 76–78, 84, 86, 115, 132, 139–40, 146, 154
English Reformation, 5
epiclesis, 50, 55–58, 157
Eternal life, 47, 50, 68, 80, 150
Eucharist/Holy Communion, 2, 5–6, 44–46, 50–60, 65–66, 76–79, 85–6, 99, 132, 139–40, 146–47, 149, 152, 155–57
Fall, the, 20, 29, 42, 64, 71

Index of Subjects

Heaven, xv, 10, 21, 31, 33–35, 37–39, 41–42, 47, 49–51, 53, 65, 67, 69–71, 78, 81, 102–3, 108, 111, 120, 125–27, 131
Hesychasm, 146
Holiness, ix, xi, 8, 21, 28–29, 31–32, 34, 40, 47–48, 57–58, 64–65, 68, 70–71, 75, 104–5, 110, 123, 125–28, 131–32, 144, 147, 157
Holy Communion/Eucharist, 6, 50–51, 54, 57, 60, 78, 128, 132, 134, 138–40, 144–45
Holy Spirit, xi, 2, 9, 11, 28–29, 35, 47, 49–50, 55–56, 61, 66, 69, 78–79, 98, 128, 132, 134, 139–41, 145
Humility, 69, 73, 81, 117, 135
Illumination, 33, 101–2, 104, 106–11, 131
Incarnation, 2, 12, 14–15, 18, 20, 22, 27, 30, 37–45, 60, 105, 131, 134, 138, 140–43, 147, 151, 155
Journal of Charles Wesley (*MSJ*), xiv, 16, 15–19, 22, 58, 86, 137, 149–50, 157
kenosis, 141–42
Knowledge, 1, 7, 9, 12, 27, 29–31, 39, 51, 65, 116, 123, 127, 134, 138, 142–44, 151
Latitudinarians, 61
Logos, 37, 67, 94, 145, 157
Love, xi, xiii, 8–12, 22, 29–30, 33, 35–36, 38, 40, 45, 48–49, 51, 54–55, 62–65, 68, 71, 73, 82, 84–85, 87–99, 101–10, 116–18, 123, 125–30, 132–34, 142–44, 146, 151, 155, 157
Methodology, 1, 40
Mystery, 8–12, 14–15, 37, 39, 41, 44, 53, 57–58, 60, 62, 85, 91, 130, 132, 141–42, 147, 151, 155
Mystic, 17, 30, 41, 75, 80–81, 84, 132, 140
Mystical theology, 4–5, 8, 13, 140, 154

Mystical union, 4, 39, 44, 142–43
Mysticism, 39, 58, 140, 145, 151, 154, 156
Nativity, 6, 30, 37–42, 105, 131, 151
Neo-Palamite school, 13
Nonjurors, 56, 58, 78, 152
Orthodox tradition, 107, 137–38, 155
Orthodoxy, 1, 3–5, 7, 9, 50, 86, 101, 128, 146–47, 149, 151, 153–55
Oxford Movement, 5, 154
Pardon, 47, 63, 68, 131
Pentecost, xiii, 28–31
Perfection, 3, 7–8, 10, 30, 42, 73, 87–88, 104, 122–28, 130, 133, 139, 151–52
perichoresis, 7,
Philokalia, 149, 155
Prayer, x, 5, 9, 11, 27, 42, 46–47, 50, 55–56, 58, 64, 66, 80–81, 90, 93, 97, 110–11, 114, 120, 124, 128, 130, 132, 133–35, 141, 143–47, 149, 151, 154
Protestant, 4, 56, 58, 84
Protestantism, 58
Redemption, xi, xiii, 21, 28, 32, 43, 71, 75, 96, 110
Religion, 16–19, 21–22, 118, 123, 131, 138, 146
Resurrection, xiii, 41–42, 44, 51, 120, 126, 143, 145, 150
Righteousness, 13–14, 21, 30, 43, 63–65, 75, 91, 103, 110–12
Sacraments, 7, 45–60, 103–4, 131, 135, 138, 140–42. *See also* Baptism; Eucharist; Holy Communion
Salvation, ix, 4, 39, 41, 46, 48, 56, 63–65, 68, 78–79, 86, 93, 124, 143, 153, 157
Sanctification, 3–4, 8, 64, 75, 122–28, 133, 135, 139, 143–44, 152
Sermons, x, xiv, 6, 16, 19–22, 47, 53, 87, 137, 149–51, 156–57
Sin(s), 30, 32–33, 46–50, 68, 80–81, 89, 91, 93–94, 103, 120, 124, 139

Index of Subjects

Soteriology, 79, 93
Theology of mystery, 8–15
theosis, ix, 2–4, 7–8, 37–40, 61, 64, 71, 86, 92, 126, 128, 136–37, 141–42, 145–47, 151–57
Transfiguration, 102, 113–20, 127
Trinity, xiii, 22, 25–27, 32, 35–36, 47, 49–50, 61–73, 79–80, 93, 100, 121, 131–32, 134, 139–40, 142–43, 146, 151

Wesleyan movement, 149–50
Wesleyan tradition, 4, 109, 126, 128, 147, 150, 154
Wisdom, xi, 10–12, 30–31, 47, 75, 123, 143–44

www.ingramcontent.com/pod-product-compliance
Lightning Source LLC
Chambersburg PA
CBHW030112170426
43198CB00009B/596